CONSTELLATIONS

Like the future itself, the imaginative possibilities of science fiction are limitless. And the very development of cinema is inextricably linked to the genre, which, from the earliest depictions of space travel and the robots of silent cinema to the immersive 3D wonders of contemporary blockbusters, has continually pushed at the boundaries. **Constellations** provides a unique opportunity for writers to share their passion for science fiction cinema in a book-length format, each title devoted to a significant film from the genre. Writers place their chosen film in a variety of contexts – generic, institutional, social, historical – enabling **Constellations** to map the terrain of science fiction cinema from the past to the present... and the future.

'This stunning, sharp series of books fills a real need for authoritative, compact studies of key science fiction films. Written in a direct and accessible style by some of the top critics in the field, brilliantly designed, lavishly illustrated and set in a very modern typeface that really shows off the text to best advantage, the volumes in the **Constellations** series promise to set the standard for SF film studies in the 21st century.'
Wheeler Winston Dixon, Ryan Professor of Film Studies, University of Nebraska

facebook Constellations

Constelbooks

Also available in this series

Blade Runner Sean Redmond

Close Encounters of the Third Kind Jon Towlson

Inception David Carter

RoboCop Omar Ahmed

Rollerball Andrew Nette

Forthcoming

12 Monkeys Susanne Kord

Children of Men Dan Dinello

Dune Christian McCrea

Jurassic Park Paul Bulloch

Mad Max Martyn Conterio

CONSTELLATIONS

THE DAMNED

Nick Riddle

auteur

Acknowledgements

For advice, correspondence and info: Professor Charles Barr, Professor Susan Felleman, David Pirie, Marcus Hearn, Dr Peter Kramer, Dr Matt Jones at De Montfort University's CATH Research Centre, Aliza James at Hammer Films.

For archive and research help, many thanks to BFI Special Collections and staff at the University of Bristol's Library Services.

Thanks also to Jez Conolly for the introduction to Auteur Publishing and many good suggestions for avenues, Bill and Avril Hammond, Graeme Hobbs, Tracy Johnson, Ira Lightman, Pam Lock, Ole Rudd, Johanna Ziegler.

Many thanks, as well, to John Atkinson at Auteur Publishing.

First published in 2019 by
Auteur, 24 Hartwell Crescent, Leighton Buzzard LU7 1NP
www.auteur.co.uk
Copyright © Auteur 2019

Series design: Nikki Hamlett at Cassels Design
Set by Cassels Design www.casselsdesign.co.uk

All rights reserved. No part of this publication may be reproduced in any material form (including photocopying or storing in any medium by electronic means and whether or not transiently or incidentally to some other use of this publication) without the permission of the copyright owner.

British Library Cataloguing-in-Publication Data
A catalogue record for this book is available from the British Library

ISBN paperback: 978-1-911325-52-9
ISBN ebook: 978-1-911325-53-6

Contents

Introduction 7
Chapter 1: The Journeyman 15
Chapter 2: The House of Sci-Fi 23
Chapter 3: 'Forward into Battle, Dear Chaps!' 29
Chapter 4: 'When the Time Comes' 41
Chapter 5: Landscape, Seascape, Manscape 47
Chapter 6: Damned Kids 57
Chapter 7: Creating Woman, Falling Man 67
Chapter 8: The Living, the Dead and the Damned 79
Chapter 9: The Heart of Darkness 89
Chapter 10: Violent Reactions and Absurd Heroics 95
Chapter 11: After-Effects 103
Appendix: Stray Elements 109
Filmography and Bibliography 115

Introduction

I didn't know what to expect when I came across a video file entitled *'These Are The Damned* (sci-fi, Losey, 1963)' on a friend's hard drive. I knew about Joseph Losey's erratic career as a blacklisted American director in exile, and as a teenager I'd seen and admired his revered Pinter collaboration *The Servant* (1963), in the days when learning about cinema outside the mainstream required tuning to BBC2 late at night. After he died in 1984, coinciding with my late-adolescent interest in arthouse films and propensity for wearing black turtlenecks, I watched all the retrospectives and read the obituaries. I heard tell of his puzzling misfires, mixed in with his impressive and sure-handed classics — for every bit of restrained brilliance like *Accident* (1966) or *The Go-Between* (1971), a florid dud like *Modesty Blaise* (1967) or an unhinged mess like *Boom!* (1968).

But *The Damned*... a *Hammer* film, as the opening credits proclaimed... I didn't recall this one in his filmography. Was this even the same Losey, the spiky intellectual who had worked with Bertolt Brecht?

The credits sequence was both reassuring and intriguing: yes, 'Director: Joseph Losey', and the austere crags of Portland Bill, with the sea beyond, established an atmosphere akin to something out of Bergman's *The Seventh Seal* (1957). When the first of Elisabeth Frink's sculptures slid into the frame, it all seemed to fit. These, probably, were the damned of the title — blasted figures whose fates were about to be explained.

But hang on. Suddenly we were on the seafront at Weymouth, dropped into a youth-culture film somewhere between *The System* (1964) and *Leather Boys* (1964). An American tourist is lured into a mugging at the hands of Oliver Reed and some ne'er-do-wells; a pair of military types help him to a local hotel where a dour Scot is arguing with a Scandinavian sculptress who... but what *is* this? A biker movie? A *Brighton Rock*-style crime flick? A drama about a Swedish artist who leaves her work on clifftops? And where's the sci-fi?

The Damned apparently perplexed many people on its release — even *before* its release, which was delayed by almost two years in England, where it finally crept

7

out without a press screening, with cuts that shortened the running time from 94 minutes to 87 in order to fit into the bottom half of a double bill with Hammer's psycho-thriller, *Maniac*. It took another two years to be released in the US, where it was cut still further to a mere 77 minutes, retitled *These Are The Damned* and paired incongruously with the critically panned historical epic *Genghis Khan* (1965). While in distribution limbo, it was screened at the 1962 Spoleto Festival, where *Films and Filming* critic John Francis Lane reported it as a piece of 'clumsy space fiction with noble pretensions that remain submerged in the heavy symbolism'. Ian Wright in *The Guardian* called it '...not a particularly good film... inarticulate, overloaded with a political message implausibly expressed'. But although many concurred with the judgement that it was unwieldy, nonetheless a certain grudging respect emerges from between the lines of many write-ups. 'It isn't a good film, but it's Wardour streets better than a lot of the old indolence to which we are weekly invited,' pronounced *The New Statesman*, its critic concluding that 'this lives at least on the level of those rare debatable films that whip up interest and surmise long after reason has tossed out the message.'[1]

The Damned won the International Science Fiction Festival's 1964 Associazione Stampa Guiliana Trieste Premio della Critica (also, and more conveniently, known as the Golden Asteroid). Some critics, moreover, were more unequivocally taken with its dark, detached view of Cold War absurdity. *The Observer*'s Philip French believed it to be 'one of the most significant recent British movies, a disturbing work of real importance'; Eugene Archer in *The New York Times* praised it as a 'bitter atomic age fantasy' that was 'chillingly effective'.

In the intervening time, its reputation languished through the 1970s and '80s — John Brosnan, in *Future Tense*, his survey of science fiction cinema, described it as 'pretentious' (1978: 115), then revised his assessment to '*very* pretentious' (1978: 149); Leslie Halliwell in his 1987 *Film Guide* called it 'Absurdly pompous, downcast and confused' — but there were always a few, such as French, the auteurist agitators of *Cahiers du Cinema* and *Movie*, or the critic and screenwriter David Pirie, to champion it. In the early 1990s, Robert Murphy, in his survey of British sixties cinema, called *The Damned* 'one of the most complex and interesting of British science fiction films' (1992: 185); Julian Petley has described it as 'a truly remarkable condemnation of both the Cold War mentality and of ruthless, institutionalised violence in general, and towards children in particular' (1999: 94). Outside academia, too, its stock has been on the ascent: *Gremlins* director and cult film buff Joe Dante holds *The Damned* aloft as 'one of the key films of the 1960s'.[2]

The film's reputation has undoubtedly risen because of its historical interest, as sixties culture continues to exert a fascination for cultural writers and consumers. Losey wanted to call it *The Brink*, and that's an apt title in more ways than he envisaged: *The Damned* was made on the cusp of the sixties, and it exists in a fold between one era and another. Pirie notes its 'interplay of all the tensions and extravagances that had punctuated the apocalyptic visions of the 1950s' (2008: 158); but it also looks to the next decade, and brazenly shakes off some of the remnants of post-war stuffiness and deference — to authority, to formula, to plot structure and tone. Its theme of surveillance and its (arguably) heroic pessimism about the power of individuals to effect change anticipated the 'political paranoia' films of the early 1970s such as *The Parallax View* (1974) and *The Conversation* (1974), and its stylised rendition of gang violence, as many have noticed, foreshadow Kubrick's use of similar imagery in *A Clockwork Orange* (1971).

In various strands of cinema history, too, *The Damned* has become a useful case study. Accounts of the British film industry by Vincent Porter and others that concentrate on the workings of companies such as Hammer, Gainsborough Pictures and Ealing Studios are often at their most colourful when dealing with examples that don't quite fit with these studios' normal practice, and are felt by the management to be rather a thorn in their side as a result (Losey in Hammer's case, and Robert Hamer, director of *Kind Hearts and Coronets* (1949), in Ealing's). Studies of the history of *mise-en-scène* and production design often hold up the work of Losey's frequent collaborator, Richard MacDonald, as a high point of the craft (though with a trajectory, many felt, that ended in excess); and in art history, the film's extensive use of the work of the British artist Elisabeth Frink has been seen by writers like Susan Felleman as pioneering, both for the seriousness with which it takes the figure of the artist and for its treatment of a female artist (2014: 107).

CONSTELLATIONS

And where *is* the sci-fi? You could say that it kicks in at the 25-minute mark, when Bernard first addresses the captive children via a video screen, or at around 49 minutes, when Henry opens the sea door with the radiation from his own body; but in another sense it's there throughout. *The Damned* is an unstable film, filled with volatile elements — from its exiled director and some of its actors to its subject matter, its uneasy mix of genres, its inconsistencies and incongruities, even some of its accents. Its central incongruity — a lethally radioactive living being that can survive its own radioactivity — is at the core of all this absurd behaviour, and far from being the 'unacceptable science fiction premise', as Losey believed, is actually, I will argue, the apotheosis of all that has gone before.

The whole film is like a science experiment, an assembly of erratic parts, like something created by Baron Frankenstein. The cause of this can be put down to several factors (a hurriedly rewritten script, for example), but ultimately, it holds up as a snapshot of a complex era of transition. *The Damned* may not be an entirely successful experiment — indeed, neither Hammer nor Columbia Pictures, with whom Hammer had a long-term US distribution deal, were willing to release the results for a while — but its influence on cinema has only grown. It's a unique film, in fact.

This book will attempt to set *The Damned* in context, or in a series of contexts: as a Joseph Losey film, as a Hammer film, as a science fiction film, as a product of the Cold War and the atmosphere of atomic terror that prevailed at the time. Its treatment of stock figures such as the scientist, the child, the artist and the 'yob' exists in a continuum, which will be sketched in each case; and some of its experiments — with imagery and ideas of living and non-living — will be examined. Its weaknesses will be impossible to ignore, but its many strengths and sources of fascination will be dwelt upon.

Having been a film postgraduate in the early 1990s, I've sworn off the 'death of the author' line of argument since its sole enduring function seems to have been to complicate matters and confuse everybody. So the word *auteur* will crop up a little, largely through Losey's privileged position (according to certain influential critics) as one of the few holders of the title in British pre-sixties cinema. But this is such a film of pieces and parts that I'm taking a range of approaches to it and looking at

The Damned

marginal aspects including its troubled production, details from the shooting script and the backgrounds of its principal cast. There are a couple of close scene analyses, but I think the cultural context is just as important as an up-close reading. Studying a film like this in any detail reveals a wide hinterland of references, whether fleeting (Thomas Hardy, umbrellas, rabbits, *Blade Runner*) or more considered (atomic radiation and mutation, Elisabeth Frink and other post-war British artists). But at the centre, always, are the children, with their influence radiating outwards like the concentric circles in diagrams of the late 1940s showing the effects of a nuclear detonation (see Chapter 4). And this is the chief source of my fascination with *The Damned*: the paradox that the children embody. The more I thought about this concept, the more I wanted look for a tradition that connects with this 'unacceptable premise'. And there definitely is one. That bit's in Chapter 8.

One angle that I'm steering clear of is Plato's 'allegory of the cave'; even though it's highly relevant to the film's themes of power, authority and education, the central conceit in *The Damned* is such a literal illustration of the allegory outlined by Plato in *The Republic* that I'm not convinced there's anything interesting to add. But it can't be entirely unacknowledged, so I'm mentioning it here.

I've tried to keep in mind a story told by the film's writer, Evan Jones, quoted in Edith DeRham's biography of Losey. He relates overhearing some French cineastes disputing the hidden profundities of a Losey film he had written:

> I listened to them and thought, 'My God, that's extraordinary! [...] I didn't mean that, and I'm sure Joe didn't either.' [...] I couldn't resist it, and said, 'Well, we actually made the film, and I think you're a bit over the top,' which made all of them furious, because they thought I was trying to put them down — I mean, by saying things like, 'the reason we ended there was because we ran out of money, actually.' That sort of thing made them even angrier. It's a game they play. (1991: 121)

Some of my claims to interpretation may seem fanciful, but I hope they're at least consistent and food for thought. I have, at any rate, tried to avoid going over the brink.

CONSTELLATIONS

Synopsis

Simon West, a retired American insurance executive, sails into Weymouth and is immediately ensnared by Joan, the sister of King, leader of a local gang who ambush and mug Simon. He is found and helped to a local hotel by two army officers, who introduce him to their superior, a government official known only as Bernard who is engaged in a secret project, and his former lover, Freya Neilson, a sculptress who rents an outhouse from him every summer to do her work.

The next day, Joan slips away from her overprotective brother to find Simon aboard his yacht, and after establishing that there are no hard feelings, the two sail out of the harbour with King and his cronies in pursuit along the shore. Simon comes on a tad strong, and Joan asks to be put ashore; she takes him to a run-down old house on the clifftop, by which time she has evidently changed her mind about him.

Meanwhile, we discover more of Bernard's project: at the Edgecliff Establishment, he presides over a team of educators and army types whose wards are a group of nine children. Bernard addresses the children via closed-circuit television, and deflects their insistent questions with vague, paternalistic reassurances that they will know more 'when the time comes'; the children, sitting at old-style school desks in a futuristic-looking classroom, are not altogether mollified.

Back at the clifftop house, Joan breaks in, explaining that this is somewhere she comes to 'hide for a while until he cools off' — meaning her brother. The sculptures make it clear that this is Freya's birdhouse. After having sex, Joan and Simon hear the approach of a car and make their escape; Freya enters, followed quickly by King, who has been tipped off about his sister's whereabouts. After a tense stand-off, King attacks one of Freya's sculptures and threatens Freya, then leaves to look for Joan.

The gang's pursuit of Simon and Joan has alerted the Edgecliff guards, and a chase over the cliffs leads to the lovers falling over the edge and landing in the water. The children rescue them and drag them into the tunnels below the cliffs where they are confined. King, meanwhile, clambers down after them.

Joan notices that the children are unnaturally cold; she and Simon are a curiosity for the children, since they're warm and adult. King is helped from the water by one of the boys, Henry, and finds the others drying off in an underground chamber. His much-vaunted violent jealousy seems to have been winded by his fall; Joan chides him and then begins to dry him with a towel.

The children, whose classroom is revealed to be part of an entire subterranean habitat, are plotting to help Simon, Joan and King by keeping them safe in their hidden tunnel. But Joan and her brother are beginning to feel ill, just as, in an intercut scene, Bernard speaks of the children's 'immunity'.

Bernard addresses the children again via the screen, demanding that they give up the adults he knows they are harbouring. The children rebel, and Bernard sends down men in radiation suits. Simon and King overpower them, and discover, using a guard's Geiger counter, that the children themselves are highly radioactive. Determined to free them, Simon, Joan and King break out of the tunnels into a sunlit quarry where Freya is looking for stone. The children taste liberty for a few moments before being rounded up again by the waiting military; Bernard informs Simon and Joan that they don't have long to live and can return to their boat, while King and the boy Henry clamber up to Freya's sports car and escape.

Pursued by helicopters, King forces Henry out of the car and drives off a bridge; Bernard explains his project more fully to an appalled Freya, and shortly thereafter shoots her. Out at sea, Simon and Joan approach their end in his boat while helicopters circle overhead.

Footnotes

1. These and other contemporary reviews were sourced either from newspapers' online archives (e.g. *Guardian, New York Times*) or from the BFI's extensive digitised collection of clippings.
2. Trailers from Hell, accessed 29-4-17 https://trailersfromhell.com/these-are-the-damned/

Chapter I: The Journeyman

The Damned is a Hammer film and a Joseph Losey film; but which is it first? I would argue that, although the auteur theory is so riddled with problems and contradictions that it can't really be called a theory at all, certain directors, by dint of personality, distinctive traits, and sheer involvement in the countless elements of the process of film-making, can be considered the guiding creative force behind a film, and therefore, for want of a better word, an auteur. Losey, by all accounts, fits the bill. Whether *The Damned* is indeed a Losey film first is debatable (and perhaps ultimately not all that important); but it's as a Losey film that we will consider it first. And since Losey's status as an auteur (in some circles at least) is of relevance to how *The Damned* has been seen, we will also briefly consider the auteur question.

Joseph Losey (1909-1984) was, and is, not an easy artist to pin down. A Midwesterner who began as a political theatre director and studied in the Soviet Union (where he met Vsevolod Meyerhold, Sergei Eisenstein and Bertolt Brecht), Losey came to film as a secondary medium, with, as his *New York Times* obituary stated, 'a feeling for language that was unusual in film directors'. His reminiscences about his childhood, in a family household of some reputation and social standing, dwell on his voracious reading habits: 'I read all of Dickens, all of Walter Scott, much of Thackeray, of Dumas,' he told Michel Ciment; 'There was an enormous library in my father's family' (1985: 15). He also loved the work of Proust, and as a child frequently stuck at home with bouts of asthma, came to identify with the pale French aesthete and 'the highly-charged and aristocratic ambience of Proust's elegant and moribund world', according to Losey biographer Edith De Rham (1991: 6).

He was, that is to say, a self-declared intellectual who strove to bring grand themes to sometimes pulpy material. He was also a contrarian, and by all accounts a somewhat difficult character: biographies of him abound with stories of furious rows and fallings-out with collaborators, producers, friends, and just about everyone else.

Was he a great director? Not everyone agrees: Pauline Kael and François Truffaut were, on the whole, less than impressed, although Kael's particular scorn was reserved for his later films, which moved her to use phrases such as 'weighty emptiness' (*Mr Klein* (1977)) and 'over furnished vacancy' (*Secret Ceremony* (1968)). Even supporters such as Gilles Jacob admitted that '[n]ot everything in his work militates in favour of consecration' (1966: 62). For example, his reliance on others to write his scripts lessens his claim to overall authorship (although he insisted that he often co-wrote screenplays uncredited), but as a visual artist (rather than a storyteller, since he often didn't seem too concerned with plot) he was capable of brilliance.

Losey's first feature, *The Boy with Green Hair* (1948), about a war orphan who wakes one morning to find that his hair has turned green overnight, establishes some of Losey's common themes and approaches: the outsider victimised by mainstream society, the brutalising effects of war and of violence in general, an expressionistic rendering of psychological states. It also, unusually for a Losey film, makes explicit reference to fears about atomic weapons (despite his avowed anti-nuclear stance, Losey rarely broke cover in his work): 'The scientists say we'll all be blown to bits in the next one,' clucks a housewife in the town store, within earshot of the boy. 'People say another war means the end of the world... Just in time to get more youngsters like Peter.'

The obvious political sympathies of *The Boy with Green Hair* only confirmed the suspicions of the House Un-American Activities Committee about Losey's leanings. He had already co-directed Brecht's *Life of Galileo* on the stage in Los Angeles and New York, and was known as a friend and/or colleague of notable lefties like the screenwriters Dalton Trumbo and Carl Foreman. After several years of embattled existence in Hollywood, Losey left the US for Europe in 1953, having been threatened with blacklisting for his Communist sympathies.

But first, he directed three *noir*ish dramas and a remake of Fritz Lang's *M* (1951). All are worth seeing; and most, despite being often uneven and not entirely convincing plotwise, have tremendous set-pieces that anticipate some of the set designs of his later British films including *The Damned*. The nocturnal manhunt in *M*, for example, is a feverish sequence full of shadows and wrought-iron staircases, clothes dummies and running figures, shot in the Bradbury Building in Los Angeles (over 30 years before Ridley Scott chose it for some key sequences in *Blade Runner*). Another, *The Prowler* (1952), features a beautifully haunting bit of set design in the final reel, when the corrupt cop Webb Garwood (Van Heflin) takes his pregnant bride to an adobe hut in a ghost town in order for her to give birth in secret. The barrenness of their surroundings both brings home to Susan (Evelyn Keyes) what she has settled for and externalises the futureless relationship that Garwood has engineered. It's also an early example of Losey's use of confined spaces to convey extreme states of mind (a precursor to the underground bunker in *The Damned*). Not for nothing did Losey become known as a major visual stylist, largely through his close working with art directors (more of which below).

Had Losey been able to remain in the States, he might have forged a Hollywood career as eclectic as that of his Wisconsin schoolmate, Nicholas Ray. His European output, beginning with the neo-realist-imitating *Imbarco a mezzanotte* (*Stranger on the Prowl*, 1952), tended to inhabit a *noir* vein, but it took a while for Losey to produce something truly memorable: *The Sleeping Tiger* (1954), *The Intimate Stranger* (1956) and *Time Without Pity* (1957) had their points of interest, and boasted some terrific performances from the likes of Leo McKern, Dirk Bogarde and Michael Redgrave, but the scripts were melodramatic and often lacked plausibility. Losey's foray into costume drama, *The Gypsy and The Gentleman* (1958), was not a happy one, as the director himself admitted to Ciment (1985: 150), but its approach to recreating the Regency period was, arguably, something new in British cinema: fastidiously researched by Losey and his designer, Richard MacDonald (see below), and shot extensively on location, a stylistic forebear of Kubrick's *Barry Lyndon* (1975).

Better by far was *Blind Date* (1959), the first of Losey's British films in which, I think, he seemed to find his feet. The first scene, in which the young artist Jan (Hardy Kruger) hops off a bus on the London Embankment with one shoe missing, seems to be tipping its hat to the breezy new style of the French New Wave. It establishes a lighter mood than one had come to expect of Losey's work; and if the rest of the film becomes a little mired in cliché (vampish mistress, adultery, murder, mistaken identity), the core two-hander between Jan and Inspector Morgan (Stanley Baker) is beautifully observed and more nuanced in terms of class and identity than most British films of the period. Losey's sympathy with the angst-ridden young painter suggests a continuity with the artist-figure so central to *The Damned*.

The Criminal (1960) continued his ascendancy, thanks in part to a decent screenplay by Alun Owen and Stanley Baker's performance as a would-be kingpin losing his status. But its success owes a lot to Losey's presentation of closed societies and levels of complicity — the prison with its inmates and warders, the criminal underworld with its mysterious dog-eat-dog hierarchy. It was another indication, following *Blind Date*, that Losey might be suited to the newly emerging, class-conscious 'vernacular' cinema that was hoving into view; indeed, around this time, according to biographer David Caute, Losey was seeking backers for an adaptation of David Storey's novel, *This Sporting Life* (1994: 280). But by the time Lindsay Anderson came to film it instead (in 1963), the movement then in full swing with the likes of *Saturday Night and Sunday Morning* (1960), *The Loneliness of the Long-Distance Runner* (1962) and *A Kind of Loving* (1962) seemed far removed from Losey's increasingly anti-realist style.

The age of the auteur

When François Truffaut and his fellow *Cahiers du Cinema* critics introduced the idea of the auteur in the mid-1950s, it was to champion the work of certain directors as distinctive, and perhaps especially to identify those working within the Hollywood studio system — such as Howard Hawks, Alfred Hitchcock and John Ford — whose singularity of outlook and vision raised their films above the generic confines of the 'industrial' film-making machine.

A good couple of years before *Village Voice* critic Andrew Sarris popularised the *Cahiers* idea in the US with his 1962 essay 'Notes on the Auteur Theory', Losey's *Time Without Pity* was released in Paris and began attracting the best reviews (in France) of his career. In September 1960, *Cahiers du Cinema* published an issue devoted to his work, reappraising his Hollywood output in glowing terms and pouring compliments on his British films.

In other words, Losey was hailed as an auteur shortly before he began production on *The Damned*. And the acclaim continued: in June 1962, the Paris Cinémathèque ran a week-long Losey retrospective, at the same time as a new magazine, *Movie*, launched in London with a Losey-themed issue and a still from *The Damned* (of King's final plunge off the bridge) on its cover. This elevation of Losey's status was far from uncontroversial, even among the *Cahiers* crowd; De Rham describes how Truffaut and Jacques Rivette compared him unfavourably to Nicholas Ray (1991: 114). But he was a major talking point in critical circles. Neil Sinyard recalls hearing an interview with Jeanne Moreau on the BBC around this time in which she placed Losey among the greatest modern film-makers:

> I was probably unaware then that what Moreau was doing was contributing to a debate that was actually one of the most heated critical issues about British cinema at this time: namely, the status of Joseph Losey. (2003: 112)

Losey was not alone as an exiled American director, nor as one who made noteworthy films in the UK: his nearest equal was probably Cy Endfield, who gave Stanley Baker two of his best roles in *Hell Drivers* (1957) and *Zulu* (1963). Others, such as Jules Dassin and John Berry, worked mostly in Europe, and Dassin in particular had some great successes, such as the much-imitated heist movie *Rififi* (1955). But there was a definite sense among certain critics that Losey was exceptional, and deserved, more than his exiled countrymen, the accolade of auteur. Discussions of the qualities that earned him this distinction tend to coalesce around his use of *mise-en-scène* — that is to say, set design, lighting, camera placement, and so on. This is probably where the strongest case for Losey's canonisation lies, and it owes its potency to his creative partnership with production designer Richard MacDonald.

Losey worked with MacDonald on 17 films, beginning with his first British production, *The Sleeping Tiger*. A graduate of the Royal College of Art, MacDonald had taught at Camberwell School of Art before moving into advertising, and was denied membership of the ACTT union as an art director for many years. As a consequence, his contributions to most of Losey's films were not only uncredited but the cause of frequent upsets on the part of whichever art director *was* officially attached to the production. Highly gifted, but by all accounts quite lacking in tact or discretion, MacDonald sometimes comes across as Losey's shadow, also forced to work in obscurity and prone to bumping up angrily against the film-making machine. Losey himself acknowledged the importance of their relationship and compared it to his previous partnership with the American art director John Hubley in Hollywood; in both cases, he told Ciment, these pairings formed 'a kind of island [...] I didn't dare to talk to anybody else [...] because of studio politics, because of unfeelingness...' (1985: 163).

MacDonald's practice of making a series of sketches of each scene, then elaborating each one with details of lighting, walls, furniture and so on, was, according to Harper and Porter, a habit he picked up from the advertising world (2003: 214). His method was also informed by his knowledge of art history, so much so that he would usually find an artist whose work served, says Caute, as a 'frame of reference' for each film: Goya for *Time Without Pity*, Rowlandson for *The Gypsy and The Gentleman*, and later, Bridget Riley and pop art for *Modesty Blaise* (1994: 322). Harper and Porter credit the pair with introducing a new way of working into the hidebound world of British film production:

> ...by a combination of determination, guile, persuasion, and brute authority, Losey and MacDonald succeeded in creating a distinctive visual style for each of their films that was markedly different to anything else in British cinema of the period. They succeeded in replacing the traditional division of labour with a narrower, more centralized and culturally orientated mode of management in which the director was able to exert almost total visual control over every shot. The age of the *auteur* had arrived. (2003: 215)

The circumstances of the filming of *The Damned*, with a good deal of exterior location shooting, afforded less malleable material for MacDonald than, say, *The Servant* would later provide. But the underground bunker and Freya's 'birdhouse', particularly, bear the stamp of a carefully thought-out design, and the surviving handful of MacDonald's sketches for the film held in the BFI archive all concern these two spaces.

Later in the 1960s, this emphasis on composition and *mise-en-scène* in Losey's films became a subject of much criticism, when his style was perceived by many as sliding into mannerism. It was *The Damned* that proved to be a watershed between his 'journeyman' genre films and his later, more 'highbrow' dramatic work. Losey followed it with the Antonioni homage *Eva* (1962) and the string of films for which he is most celebrated, including the Pinter-scripted *The Servant* (1963), *Accident* (1967) and *The Go-Between* (1971). These later films fall outside the bounds of this book, but they're worth keeping in mind; an auteur who doesn't revisit and reuse images and ideas compulsively is barely an auteur at all.

Science fiction and the auteur

One of Losey's French champions, Gilles Jacob, described his output up to the early 1960s as 'a series of experiments constantly redirected towards a more precise understanding of his art' (1966: 62) — an interesting phrase in the context of this book's approach to *The Damned* as a kind of wayward experiment. Jacob goes on to observe in Losey's style 'a sort of abstraction, a laboratory chill in the construction of the characters', and concludes: 'Because they have been carefully and patiently cultivated in the test-tube, they lack the freedom of life' (1966: 62). It's an assessment also strikingly applicable to the nine child-characters in *The Damned*.

I think his work became even chillier and more abstracted through the sixties and beyond, but where *The Damned* sits along this spectrum is open to debate. The empathy that Losey showed with the eponymous green-haired boy in his first feature is now more dispersed, largely because we experience the nine children as more of a group, and one that can't help but give off an all-too-literal 'laboratory chill'. But there's definitely a lowering of the emotional temperature as well; science fiction (pre-*Star Wars* (1977) at least) is prone to the odd ice crystal or two, especially when practiced by directors who loosely inhabit the auteur category. It's not the shiny technology, which most arthouse directors don't seem to favour anyway. It's the cerebral tendencies that the genre tends to draw out in this kind of film-maker, and perhaps the fact that auteurs tend only to try science fiction once, as a kind of experiment (to echo Jacob's pronouncement on Losey). Contemporary reviews often take these films to task using similar language: see, for example, Bosley Crowther on *Fahrenheit 451* (1966) ('pretentious and pedantic'), Arthur M Schlesinger, Jr on *2001: A Space Odyssey* (1968) ('morally pretentious, intellectually obscure and inordinately long'); or Roger Ebert on *The Man Who Fell to Earth* (1976) ('preposterous and posturing'). *The Damned*, too, was criticised as pretentious.[3]

CONSTELLATIONS

But there's a dimension to Losey's film that runs counter to this abstractedness: a common longing to connect. These pairings proliferate: Joan and Simon, Freya and Bernard, Henry and King, Sid and Freya, even King and Freya. Repeated viewings make these moments of attraction increasingly poignant — a word one doesn't often reach for when discussing a Losey film. But then *The Damned* is a strange film in the Losey canon, in the science fiction genre, and (as we're about to see) in the Hammer catalogue.

Footnotes

3. Comments from these reviews of other science fiction films by 'auteurs' were sourced from the Wikipedia entries for the film concerned.

Chapter 2: The House of Sci-Fi: Hammer and Science Fiction

On the face of it, Losey was not a natural choice to direct a film for Hammer; the company favoured tried-and-tested directors such as Val Guest and Terence Fisher. But neither were Losey and Hammer unacquainted with each other: Hinds had hired him on the suggestion of his friend, the blacklisted writer Carl Foreman, to direct a short divertissement for Hammer, *A Man on the Beach* (1955), so he was not an unknown quantity, and he had been brought back to direct *X the Unknown*, until either illness or politics intervened (see below). Losey's comments about the studio's output were hardly warm — he told Ciment of his distate for the 'overt violence' in many of their scripts (1985: 199), but in an interview with Penelope Houston in *Sight and Sound* he also professed his admiration for at least one of their regular directors, Seth Holt (1961:184). In the relatively small filmmaking community in the UK, Losey must also have had other connections with Hammer; his cinematographer on *Time Without Pity*, for example, was Freddie Francis, who became one of Hammer's regular directors in the 1960s.

Hammer had become, by 1963, an easy studio to pin down: the broader production slate of the 1950s had been narrowed to mainly produce (jointly with US partners, mostly Columbia and Universal) Gothic horror and modern thriller/slasher films, with little interest in cultural 'respectability'. The declaration, quoted by Vincent Porter, of its managing director, James Carreras, that 'I'm prepared to make Strauss waltzes tomorrow, if they'll make money' (1983: 192) conveys something of the market-led philosophy at Hammer, but doesn't do justice to the craftsmanship and style of their best work (except that Strauss, too, was accomplished at producing generic pieces with artistry and flair). But until a few years previously, the company's repertoire had been far broader.

Since Hammer's first feature-length film, *The Mystery of the Mary Celeste* (1935), its slate of releases covered a multitude of subjects and genres: mysteries (*Doctor Morelle*, (1949), *Whispering Smith Hits London* (1952)), comedies (*What the Butler Saw, The Lady Craved Excitement* (both 1950)), crime dramas and noirs (*Cloudburst* (1951), *The Last Page* (1952)) — and science fiction, a genre in which Hammer's first, rather faltering, entries were *Four-Sided Triangle* and *Spaceways* (both 1953).

These two make for an interesting pair, demonstrating two distinct science fiction traditions. *Four-Sided Triangle* is a *Frankenstein*-inspired doppelgänger tale (partly shot in Weymouth) in which a besotted young scientist creates a duplicate of his best friend's fiancée, with predictably tragic results; the second is a murder mystery with spacesuits, adapted from a BBC radio drama. Neither of them did great business, and after a deal with an American company, Robert Lippert Productions, ended in 1955, Hammer produced almost nothing for a year. But the company's next attempt at science fiction changed its fortunes.

The Quatermass Xperiment (1955), which condensed Nigel Kneale's ground-breaking 1953 BBC TV serial into a brisk sci-fi horror yarn, hit a nerve with the viewing public. It wasn't a rocket-ships-and-romance confection: it was dark stuff (emphasised by Hammer's playing up its 'X' certificate in the title), dealing in contagion, mutilation, and the slow transformation of a man, the astronaut Victor Carroon (Richard Wordsworth), into a monstrous alien creature. Professor Quatermass (played by the American actor Brian Donlevy) is a bit of a monster himself, callous and irascible, unmoved by the fate of the man he sent into space. Modern science, the film suggests, risks not just damaging the human body but also compromising the humanity and decency for which, a decade earlier, it helped to fight.

X the Unknown (1956) was planned as a sequel to *The Quatermass Xperiment*, but Kneale, already put out by some of the changes Hammer had made to his TV script and by the casting of Donlevy, refused to allow the use of the Quatermass name for the new film. It is Dr Royston (Dean Jagger), therefore, who is summoned to investigate a strange outbreak of lethal radioactivity in a Scottish quarry and discovers an ancient subterranean life-form that feeds on radiation.

The director originally appointed to *X the Unknown* was, in fact, Joseph Losey, having proved himself with *A Man on the Beach*. He got as far as scouting locations before being replaced by Leslie Norman; the official reason was a bout of pneumonia, but the more commonly accepted theory is that Dean Jagger, whose politics were violently anti-Communist, insisted on Losey's removal.

The Damned

What Losey would have made of *X the Unknown* is uncertain; on the face of it, there wouldn't have been a lot for him to get his teeth into. Moreover, the idea of sentient radioactive mud from the Earth's core is just as preposterous as the central conceit that he took such exception to in *The Damned*. Jimmy Sangster's script is efficient, not stopping to dwell on injustice, class, emotional conflict, or the playing out of complex ideas. The soldiers on exercise at the beginning are music-hall types, ribbing each other and complaining about army food; Dr Royston is bluff but courteous, a scientist-detective without the dangerous arrogance of Donlevy's Quatermass. As for an outsider figure, the closest candidate, besides Royston, is the radioactive life-form itself; perhaps Losey, who demonstrated such sympathy for the child-murderer in his remake of *M*, might have found rich material there, or in the mutated Carroon in *The Quatermass Xperiment*, had he been its director.

The opening sequence of *X the Unknown*, however, bears an inescapable similarity to that of *The Damned*: the camera pans across a bleak, barren landscape, over James Bernard's terse, string-dominated score. The meaning is clear: this is about the earth, the land, and what lies beneath it (especially when a soldier with a Geiger counter comes into frame). *The Damned*, too, seems to announce its subject with its opening pan, and becomes similarly concerned with matters subterranean.

The success of *X the Unknown* in the US — something that might have been harmed had Losey's name been attached to it — created an appetite for more. Hammer acquired the rights to Kneale's own *Quatermass* sequel, broadcast by the BBC in 1955, and agreed to bring Kneale himself in to adapt the script. The result, *Quatermass 2* (1957), shows popular faith in the establishment beginning to show signs of strain.

Following a mysterious hail of meteorites in the middle of the English countryside, Quatermass discovers a large-scale facility, supposedly a food-processing plant, under construction there, and bearing a strange resemblance to his own plans for a lunar colony which were rejected by the government. His assistant is infected by spores from one of the meteorites and is marched off by armed guards. Quatermass makes representation to the corridors of power, but discovers that at least one high-ranking Whitehall mandarin has been infected and 'turned' by the alien intelligence, along with whole swathes of the army; Members of Parliament visit the facility, only to prove impotent against a sinister conspiracy. Finally, and interestingly, given that 1957 also saw the release of Hammer's first Frankenstein film, *The Curse of Frankenstein*, local villagers armed with improvised weapons march as a mob on the plant and break down the gates. Quatermass, realising that the alien creatures need their own life support system to protect them from the Earth's atmosphere, floods them with oxygen and destroys them.

Quatermass 2 shows another step in the erosion of public trust in authority. But we've only come so far; the threat still comes from outside, from the non-human Other. Once we've entered Bernard's bunker on Portland Bill, we don't need alien intervention to produce monsters. Kneale was entirely in sympathy with this idea: witness his own adaptation of George Orwell's *Nineteen Eighty-Four* for BBC Television (1954).

On the matter of science in the post-war era, it was *The Curse of Frankenstein* that delivered one of the most damning verdicts. Baron Frankenstein (Peter Cushing), in his quest for the highest-quality body parts with which to make his creature, invites the renowned Professor Bernstein (Paul Hardtmuth), 'the greatest brain in Europe', to dinner. After various pleasantries, the Professor is moved to hold forth on morality: 'There's a great difference between knowing that a thing is so and knowing how to use that knowledge for the good of mankind.' Frankenstein looks discomfited by this prick to his conscience, but Bernstein continues:

> The trouble with us scientists is we quickly tire of our discoveries. We hand them over to people who are not ready for them, while we go off again into the darkness of ignorance, searching for other discoveries which will be mishandled in just the same way when the time comes.

A few minutes later, the Professor is dead and his peerless brain is destined for a new cavity, but he has summed up perfectly the modern anxiety about scientific progress — and that final phrase, 'when the time comes', resonates all the way to Bernard's underground bunker in *The Damned*.

Mixing it up

A certain amount of commentary on the *The Damned* has identified it as an anomaly in the Hammer catalogue. There's its frequent description as a kind of hybrid, mixing the biker/delinquent movie with the science fiction genre; but as Harper and Porter point out, Hammer had previous form in this department. They cite the example of *The Glass Cage* (1955), which combines a reading of Kafka's story 'A Hunger Artist' with references to circus films such as Tod Browning's *Freaks* (1932), and describe it as 'an important indication of the unpredictable oddness of Hammer's hybrid films' (2003: 143). The genre mix in *The Damned* is more ungainly than most because, rather than running concurrently throughout the film, the genres tend to interrupt each other. This is, I think, largely a consequence of the hurried nature of Jones' rewrite; with more time, perhaps the genres would have been woven a little more smoothly together. Even so, this kind of disruption was hardly unique in early-sixties cinema: Hitchcock delighted in wrong-footing audiences with narrative and stylistic rifts, most notably in *Psycho* (1960).

The mixing of genres (*Four-Sided Triangle* is another example, with its mashup of *Frankenstein* and romantic drama) would also be an exhibit in the prosecution's case against Hammer as a purveyor of unrealistic, non-naturalistic, and therefore un-British, cinema. As Pirie and many others have pointed out, the taste-makers and gatekeepers of British cinema's canonical mainstream have long prized a realist, documentary-inspired aesthetic and held the fantastical and the visionary in contempt; as Pirie writes, 'there is in Britain's official culture an enormous historical prejudice in favour of material that may be termed loosely "realism"', and this prejudice 'demands that the subject itself directly reflects present social conditions, that it has a documentary contemporary feel and avoids anything too imaginative or "other"' (2002: 10). For instance, John Grierson was once favoured over Powell and Pressburger and, says Pirie, strove to talk Alfred Hitchcock out of making genre pictures (2002: 11).

For the first *Quatermass* film, director Val Guest chose to mitigate the far-fetched nature of the story by opening the film in a 'realist' style, with newsreel-type footage of emergency services swinging into action. This approach, although not unprecedented in science fiction and fantasy (the most famous contemporary example is Orson Welles' *War of the Worlds* radio broadcast in 1938), was untypical, and really, *Quatermass* is also a hybrid: documentary jostles with fantasy, and Carroon is the tragic embodiment of hybridity. One can even interpret his 'rampage' as an allegory of science fiction itself: a despised, unnatural genre, censured by the establishment and finally containable only by a bastion of British morality like Westminster Abbey.

But here's where Losey, for all his supercilious remarks about fable and populist forms of entertainment, doesn't seem like such a strange choice of director for a Hammer film. The development of his style began with the social-realist documentary of *A Child Went Forth* (1941) and *Youth Gets a Break* (1941) only for his films to become art-directed within an inch of their lives by the time he shot *The Servant*. But he *always* had a tendency towards hybridity, from the neorealist/film noir *Stranger on the Prowl* to the musical/comedy/spy drama *Modesty Blaise*.

Hammer's problems with Losey, however, were very real. They began early on in pre-production, and lasted a good year or two after shooting finished. Not every study of a film benefits from an account of its making, but *The Damned*, I think, does; for in Losey's strange science experiment, this is where its elements start to collide and combine.

Chapter 3: 'Forward into Battle, Dear Chaps': The Production

'The whole battle of getting films done — and it *is* a battle all the time...'
Joseph Losey, interview with Tom Milne (1968: 34)

Gestation

When asked by Michel Ciment how different the screenplay was from HL Lawrence's book, Losey replied, not altogether accurately: 'Completely. The only thing that came from the book was the gang of boys' (1985: 198). Most subsequent accounts take up this angle. It's surprising, then, to read the novel and find many of the film's core ideas and elements present and correct.

Henry Lionel Lawrence (1908-1990) published only two novels: *The Sparta Medallion* (1961), a thriller about Nazis in South America, and before that, *The Children of Light* (1960), a briskly paced, dystopian story set in southern England in some near future — and *surely* influenced by a viewing of a Quatermass tale or two and a reading of John Wyndham. It's no masterpiece, but in the context of the film it's worth visiting in *précis*.

Simon Largwell, an architect, accidentally kills his unfaithful wife and flees from London to Brighton, Shoreham, then Southampton, where he falls foul of a street gang who call themselves the Borgias (or sometimes the Poisoners). Their leader, Caesar, is in the midst of some titillatingly described nastiness with Joan, who is later revealed to be his half-sister, when Simon is hauled in by a couple of henchmen. After getting a beating — a rather worse one than the film's Simon is subjected to — he is thrown out of a moving car, only to be found later by Joan, who also jumped from the car to escape her murderous brother. They go on the run together, and stumble across some fenced-off Ministry of Defence property, where they break in and fall down a shaft.

Bernard, in his office in Whitehall, receives word that 'Project Mannekin' has had a break-in, and instructs that the press be given a cover story about the two fugitives having blundered into a minefield. But local journalist Johnny Parks doesn't buy it.

Simon and Joan wake up in hospital beds, having been taken care of by a group of precocious children, all of whom have pure white hair. Meanwhile, Johnny Parks has gone to the military base to investigate for himself and finds Simon and Joan with the children. Having brought a Geiger counter, he discovers the high amounts of radiation, but not the source, and the three adults begin their escape to tell the outside world about the imprisoned children. One of them, Sylvia, follows them out, and they decide to take her to a London newspaper, the *Comet*. Their flight is tracked by Crane, a henchman of Bernard's, who, encountering and dispensing with Caesar along the way, intercepts Simon and Joan and delivers them to Bernard. Bernard delivers the full explanation about the radioactive children, the future of mankind, and so on.

On the way to the London newspaper, Johnny Parks and Sylvia are involved in a fatal accident on Westminster Bridge. In a sealed-off hospital ward, Simon and Joan share their last moments together. And a few weeks later, in the offices of the *Comet*, the News Editor wonders whether, then decides not, to look further into the strange incidents that led to the death of the reporter.

The Children of Light is itself something of a hybrid: clearly it owes something to 'on-the-run' novels such as John Buchan's *The Thirty-Nine Steps*, but its tone is much darker. There's a bit of *Brighton Rock* in its depiction of a criminal gang lurking in a bombed-out area of Southampton, and its secret-experiments scenario, as mentioned, conjures up *Quatermass*. Lawrence even gives his 'eminence grise' the same first name as Nigel Kneale's Professor.

The title is taken from a New Testament passage reprinted at the front of the novel ('For the children of this world are in their generation wiser than the children of light' — Luke, xvi. 8), but doesn't, I think, stand up to any literal exegesis. The passage is from the Parable of the Unjust Steward, which famously concludes that 'No servant can serve two masters' — a phrase that could loosely be applied to Bernard, the bureaucrat of whom Freya observes that 'A public servant is the only servant who has secrets from his master'. But really, the novel's title seems to be more of a riff on connotations to do with radiation, innocence and guilt. That said, it's worth observing that the title conjures up the moral opposite of that suggested by the film's eventual title. Unless one feels like hazarding a tenuous link via the name Lucifer ('Bearer of light')...

The Damned retains, or reworks, a good deal more of the source novel than Losey suggested: the names of the principal characters (with a relegation for the head thug from Caesar to mere King), the youth gang, the love story, the southern-England setting, the irradiated, bunker-bound children, the helicopter as malign pursuer, the patriarch committing horrors in the name of human survival. The novel is set in the future — although, strangely, it takes quite some time to tell us, and then only drops hints, with references to things like a Mars rocket — but the tone and the imagery are still steeped in World War II (which the film notably isn't), with bombed ruins and a down-at-heel air to everything. Atomic testing has so destabilised the planet's environment that mass sterility is imminent. The threat, therefore, comes not from a future atomic war that the film's Bernard considers inevitable, but from a global catastrophe, caused by nuclear testing, which is already unfolding as the novel opens. This aspect, and the sizeable amount of newspaper-man talk, gives the book a more-than-passing resemblance to Val Guest's *The Day the Earth Caught Fire* (1961), which also uses World War II and the Blitz as reference points (albeit with a strong indication that the Blitz spirit won't help in the next conflagration — an argument seconded by the downbeat ending of *The Damned*).

The Damned was criticised for its bleakness, but if anything, *The Children of Light* is bleaker still. The criminal gang are almost feral compared to King's rather tame bikers: 'cruel, vicious, despairing faces' (1960: 158), with a leader, in contrast to Oliver Reed's well-fed King, 'a small, skinny figure with a face almost bare of flesh' (1960: 19). And you'd never get this lot to march in formation, parodically or otherwise: they lash out at each other at the merest provocation, and Caesar is all but devoured by his underlings after being struck down. His treatment of Joan is far more explicitly sadistic and sexual, too, and not in the least motivated by some misguided protective impulse.

The book's action is played out in a larger space, as the press become involved and one of the children is smuggled to London; but the fugitives are either killed in a staged 'accident' on Westminster Bridge or left to fade away in a secret hospital ward. Representatives of the press are shown raising an eyebrow at the very end, but in a resigned sort of way. The human race, moreover, is doomed: every man on the planet will soon be firing blanks.

Mutation

How did *The Children of Light*, a novel that crept out from a minor publisher and scarcely troubled the marketplace, attract the attention of Hammer? Conventional wisdom has it that executive producer Michael Carreras, often keen to broaden Hammer's range, set things in motion. But not so: David Pirie discovered a letter in the Hammer archives, sent from a businessman friend of Lawrence's (one Ernest Simon) to another acquaintance, James Carreras. In the letter, dated 5 November 1960, Simon insisted that the book 'would make a sensational film' and offered to 'have a copy delivered to you'. Carreras senior took him up on the offer and passed the book to Anthony Hinds, who agreed that there was mileage in it. Losey's and Michael Carreras' remarks on the production do seem to foreground the latter's involvement over that of Hinds, a naturally self-effacing character who, says Pirie, 'preferred to keep well in the background' (2008: 52).

James Carreras may have been drawn by the novel's *Quatermass*-like elements such as the secret facility; but a more obvious appeal, as Pirie points out, would have been the book's precocious, eerie children, giving it 'an unmistakable resemblance to *Village of the Damned* which had been a big hit that year (much to James Carreras' irritation, for Hammer had missed out on the rights)'. The title change to *The Damned* confirms this reasoning: 'James Carreras would never pass up the chance of a title that was pre-sold' (2008: 155).

There was considerable back-and-forth over the script. Lawrence himself had insisted on adapting his novel, and the sample pages that he sent to Hinds were, in the latter's words, not 'quite good enough', but probably, Hinds felt, adequate basis for a screenplay co-written 'between Lawrence, the director and myself.' This, however, was before Losey provisionally agreed to direct in February 1961. Losey declared his unhappiness with the Lawrence-Hinds draft of the screenplay and suggested bringing in Ben Barzman, his old comrade-in-arms who had co-written his first feature, *The Boy with Green Hair*.

Having been named by the director Edward Dmytryk in front of the House Un-American Activities Committee in 1951, Barzman and his wife had moved to Europe, becoming part of a community of exiles that also included directors John Berry and Jules Dassin. Losey had subsequently recruited him to write the screenplay for his Italian film *Stranger on the Prowl* (1952), and then for *Time Without Pity* and *Blind Date* in Britain. Barzman had previous form as far as writing science fiction was concerned; in 1960 he had published a novel, *Out of this World* (US title *Twinkle, Twinkle Little Star*), a quite intriguing story about the discovery of a twin planet Earth with a parallel history, except that World War II never happened. In this novel, too, the science fiction element only appears part-way through.

Hinds agreed to commission a rewrite from Barzman, whom Losey went to visit, according to Caute, in the south of France to work on the screenplay with him (1994: 142). In due course, Barzman submitted a script that preserved the man-on-the-run premise, updated the gang to Teddy Boys, introduced the figure of the sculptor (presumably at the urging of Losey) and — controversially — had Simon raping Joan at the artist's house.

That we know anything of the Barzman script (although a copy may be squirrelled away with Evan Jones' papers, currently in a sealed archive in Oxford's Bodleian Library) is down to the British Board of Film Classification (BBFC), whose script reader on duty that day, Audrey Field, wrote a synopsis. Her comments on *The Children of Light* are scathing, dimissive and rather supercilious. 'It seems that the people behind this project are against Teddy Boys, "The Establishment" and the nuclear deterrent,' she tutted. 'What they are in favour of is less easy to guess, though it seems likely that they are ardent fellow travellers or fully paid up members of the Communist party...' (2002: 218).

These were strong words from an ostensibly apolitical body, and raise doubts about Field's level of knowledge about Losey and Barzman's treatment at the hands of HUAC. But politics aside, Hammer's relations with the BBFC by this stage were becoming strained. Besides censor-baiting stunts like releasing pictures that boasted their X rating in their titles, Hammer were also a conspicuous example of the kind of outfit being viewed with opprobrium in the wake of the hoo-ha over Michael Powell's *Peeping Tom* (1960). Producers were going too far, in the view of moral guardians such as John Trevelyan, Secretary of the BBFC, who, according to Denis Meikle, appears to have tried to stop Hammer from making horror films at all (1996: 107).

Of the Barzman script, Field (as quoted by Kinsey) continues:

> Anyway, we cannot concern ourselves with the ideas, which in any case escape the sort of 'X' film patrons we want to protect! The worry here is the unhappy Mr King and friends with the bicycle chains (and one or two other bits of nasty violence). The makers of the film are doubtless right in saying that it ought to be 'X', though the reason they give (ie, that it is a 'very adult subject') is perhaps not very sound: the bits that would appeal to morons of violent inclinations are much more undesirable for children. I think myself that the story is a lot of symbolic claptrap, though I don't deny that some of the radioactive cavern stuff may have a weird force and power (it is certainly not much more incredible than the behaviour of the characters in the outside world!). (2002: 218)

One could base a thesis on Field's full report and what it indicates about the establishment's attitude in the early 1960s to public morals, audience susceptibility and comparative intelligence ('The sort of "X" film patrons we want to protect' are 'morons of violent inclinations' who would fail to grasp 'the ideas'? Some of this sounds a little like Bernard's patronising sermons to the children). But the BBFC's disapproval, its stern exchange of correspondence with James Carreras and Tony Hinds, and its itemised list of points in the script 'which are likely to be troublesome in the completed film', were overtaken by the chaotic juggernaut of Losey's own machinations. For, with no warning, the director declared the Barzman script to be unworkable, and insisted that he be allowed to bring in a new writer, Evan Jones, to draft a new screenplay.

Jones was born in Portland, Jamaica and, after spending his college years in Pennsylvania and working at a refugee camp in Palestine, studied at Wadham College, Oxford. Losey's invitation to Jones, says Caute, was issued on the strength of his play, *In a Backward Country*, (1994: 149) and Losey felt, as he told Ciment, 'a certain political kinship' with him (1985: 198). Jones' involvement finally gives Losey some propulsion away from the film noir archetypes and idioms that the likes of Barzman brought to their screenplays. Jones adds a new quality to the material: a playwright's sensibility. One can see this in, for example, the scene between Sid and Freya towards the end of the film; in terms of plot, it has no business being there, but it contributes to the layer of poignancy that I mentioned earlier. Jones permits himself the leisure of a conversation that explores Sid's impulse to connect without requiring a resolution.

There's some disagreement among the sources on the timing involved in Jones' arrival. Kim Newman quotes Michael Carreras' claim that Losey left it 'something like twenty-four hours before we were going to shoot the film' (1999: 166); in historian Wayne Kinsey's version (for which he had access to Hammer correspondence), Losey issued his demand two weeks before principal photography (2002: 221), and it was during those two weeks that Jones reshaped the screenplay.

Perhaps this is splitting hairs; two weeks or 24 hours, Losey's ultimatum was still, as Carreras described it, 'very naughty' (1999: 166). But the inconsistencies continue: Denis Meikle recounts that, after this bombshell, 'Tony Hinds was horrified and, true to form, he promptly disappeared from the scene. Carreras... had to pick up the reins...' (1996: 118). Losey's own recollection, too, follows this notion. But among the stills in the BFI's Losey archive is a shot of Alexander Knox on location in Weymouth, deep in discussion with Hinds; and Kinsey quotes a diary entry by Harry Oakes, focus puller on the production, about an exchange he had with Hinds on Portland Bill (2002: 222). This lends further support to Pirie's contention that Hinds was a far greater, and more overlooked, creative force at Hammer than Carreras. This is a view echoed by Sue Harper and Vincent Porter, who call Hinds 'the most "hands-on" producer in the cinema of the decade' (2003: 137).

Whichever version of events you choose to believe, it still left Jones with a rush job on his hands. In an interview with Gordon Gow for *Films and Filming*, Losey later recalled:

> We were working on the script while we were in the process of shooting; although

Evan Jones was marvellous to work with and almost killed himself putting things together every night. This method of working can have its advantage [...] but when it's an absolute necessity because you haven't got a satisfactory script before you start shooting — well then it becomes very hard on everybody: writer and director and actors. (1971: 39)

Losey's copy of the shooting script, kept in the BFI archives, confirms this seat-of-the-pants impression. The pages are arranged in four different colours — white, yellow, pink and blue — and heavily annotated in pencil; and the top layer (white), although marked 'SHOT WHITE SCRIPT (as at 18 June)', begins halfway through the early scene at the Gloucester Hotel with some dialogue that didn't make it to the final film. Reading the script in a linear fashion is impossible: the order jumps around, and new pages are often inserted (having been feverishly typed by Jones overnight, one assumes), with old sections of dialogue and description crossed out in an effort to maintain continuity. A person suspicious of Losey's motives might suspect him of deliberately ordering last-minute rewrites *in order* to produce a jumbled screenplay that only he could keep track of. In any case, the shooting script is an incongruous map to a film stuffed with incongruities.

Included are a few short scenes that, one assumes, were shot but then cut later. Some are just bridging scenes of little or no consequence, such as Major Holland and Captain Gregory's discovery of the beaten-up West in the Weymouth backstreet (although there are character descriptions included that emphasise their class differences: Holland is from 'common origins'; Gregory is 'better educated, but not so common nor so tough'). A couple of the cut scenes shed more light on the characters' relation to one another, and I'll bring those up at what seems the relevant point.

On the top sheet of the yellow layer, a note reads:

> The style of the picture is realistic, but with a continuous overtone of irony, even of caricature. It is always a little larger than life, more savage, more terrifying, and more full of hope.

This is an interesting statement of intent, mostly realised; but 'full of hope'? Debatable, to say the least. We'll come back to that in Chapter 10.

Production

Since it's useful in an experiment to know something of the properties of its elements, let's acquaint ourselves with the principal actors, who convened with the director and crew in Weymouth in May 1961.

MacDonald Carey, an American actor who had been the male lead in Losey's second feature, *The Lawless*, could hardly be described as stand-out hero material. Tellingly, one of Carey's career highlights had been a role in *The Great Gatsby* (1949) as Nick Carraway, the story's unobtrusive (i.e. bland) narrator. But his casting followed the playbook for low-budget UK-US co-productions of the era: put a familiar but relatively cheap American star in the role of hero (Howard Duff in *Spaceways*, Dean Jagger in *X the Unknown*, Brian Donlevy in *Quatermass* and *Quatermass 2*).

Oliver Reed had already appeared, mostly uncredited, in several Hammer films, along with minor roles in lightweight comedies like *The Square Peg* and *The Captain's Table* (both 1959), but he had come to prominence as the lead in Hammer's *The Curse of the Werewolf* (1961), playing the doomed young Leon Corledo with an anguished intensity that brought him to public attention. *The Damned* gave Reed his second leading role, one of a succession with Hammer that amounted to 'a concerted campaign' designed 'to groom him for stardom,' according to Denis Meikle (1996: 107).

Shirley Anne Field had worked up from extra and walk-on roles in the mid-1950s through supporting turns in comedies like *Man in the Moon* (1960) to more substantial dramatic parts in *The Entertainer* (1960) and *Saturday Night and Sunday Morning* (1960). Reed's and Field's progression ran parallel during these years: they'd been cast in the same film twice before, in *Upstairs and Downstairs* (1959) and *Beat Girl* (1960) (in the latter as two of the era's least convincing beat-obsessed teens). Losey complained to Ciment that she had been imposed upon him by Columbia 'because she had just played with Olivier and had had some kind of success so they thought she was a star' (1985: 198).

Canadian-born Alexander Knox had, according to De Rham, known Losey in New York (1991: 123) and moved to England twice — once in the 1930s, when he became one of the first actors on BBC radio, and again after being 'greylisted' for his leftist views and activities such as co-founding the Committee of the First Amendment. He had played one of the leads in Losey's first British film, *The Sleeping Tiger*, as another Celtic authority figure with a misguided sense of mission, but this time devoted to freeing his young charge, not incarcerating him.[4]

Viveca Lindfors was a Swedish actress whose Hollywood CV included one of Errol Flynn's last swashbucklers, *Adventures of Don Juan* (1948), and Fritz Lang's *Moonfleet* (1955), which was set, like its source novel, a stone's throw from Portland Bill (but shot in California). Losey would have known Lindfors through her husband, the playwright George Tabori, whom he knew from his time directing Brecht's *Galileo* in Los Angeles. Lindfors is the film's great strength, performance-wise, and her character provides a much-needed counterpoint to the others; but Losey looked back on his experiences directing her with mixed feelings.

The location shooting was not without incident: the stuntman who drove King's car off the causeway barely escaped with his life, and a key scene between Lindfors and Knox brought out their contrasting acting styles so starkly that the method-trained Lindfors drove the more traditional Knox to distraction. 'Then she had a nervous breakdown and began to shiver and shake and I got blankets and wrapped her up and fed her half a bottle of brandy,' the gallant Losey told Michel Ciment. 'Then we had the scene' (1985: 203).

This little vignette, unsurprisingly, doesn't make it into Lindfors' memoir, *Viveka... Viveca* (1981). Of the five principals in *The Damned*, four published memoirs (Knox wrote novels and essays on acting but no memoir); only one, Shirley Anne Field, mentions *The Damned* at any length. She recounts several incidents on location — including being left for hours by the crew in a ravine with Reed and Carey when the light changed — but the most notable passage, in terms of the finished film, concerns her performance ('indifferent' says critic Philip French; 'just awful' was Losey's rather ungracious comment (1985: 198)). It's worth mentioning here, and not just because it helps to explain her admittedly rather wooden manner. Field recalls that, at this early stage in her career, she had become 'very self conscious of the way I sounded' after having drawn criticism over her previous roles, and so, 'in self-defence, I adopted a flat monotone. As a result, my acting was not as free as it should have been' (1991: 133).

But some of this awkwardness is written into the role. The shooting script explains that she 'feels penned in by her circumstances' (rather as Field felt restricted by hers), and Joan does seem to take her cues from her surroundings, talking like a tough street kid while with King and the gang and then becoming quite lyrical (and losing her street accent) while on the run with West — so much so that he remarks on it. In the novel, Joan is equally mutable: her behaviour, even her vocabulary, change after she runs away with Simon. And this arguably suits the texture of the film, just as their romantic involvement, otherwise pretty unbelievable, fits a certain pattern: this is a story packed with mutations and incongruities in an anomaly of a film. Adding to this impression of unevenness is Field's recollection that most of their dialogue had to be dubbed later because of wind noise on location (1991: 134).

Interior scenes were shot at Hammer's Bray Studios, and the film wrapped on 22 June. But there were further problems — not so much with the BBFC this time (Kinsey states that their only requirement was the removal of a shot of King striking an out-of-frame Simon with his umbrella during the mugging (2002: 239)), but with Hammer and Columbia. Hinds had two principal demands: that Losey reduce the incestuous overtones of the King/Joan relationship by filming a new scene, and that Freya's murder should be carried out by Bernard and not an unknown gunman in the helicopter. Losey initially won Columbia's support to refuse these demands, but eventually, says Hearn, he was 'persuaded to shoot a new scene [...] in an amusement arcade' between Field and Reed. The insert showing Bernard firing the fatal shot was also filmed, without Losey's involvement (2010: 11).

I've already described the film's ignominious treatment in the marketplace — its consignment to limbo, a little like Bernard's children, waiting for their time to come. In the meantime, developments in the Cold War would make the themes of *The Damned* more timely than ever.

Footnotes

4. Biographical details for Alexander Knox were mostly sourced from the Northern Stars website: www.northernstars.ca/knox_alexander_bio. Accessed 30-4-17

Chapter 4: 'When The Time Comes': *The Damned* and British Cold War Culture

British cinema was far slower than Hollywood to address the nuclear threat in the wake of Hiroshima and Nagasaki; one of the few British films before the 1950s to tackle nuclear weapons was Hammer's own *Dick Barton Strikes Back* (1949), the second of its three adaptations of the BBC radio serial, though needless to say the subject received fairly light treatment.

This was a reflection of the government's own reticence on the matter. As historian Tony Shaw points out, the Attlee government began a nuclear weapons programme in 1947 under great secrecy: 'Parliament was told the minimum about the nation's atomic energy and weapons developments, and MPs considered it "indecent" to ask about them' (2006: 117). Presidents Truman and Eisenhower, on the other hand, showered the American public with information though the Atoms for Peace initiative, to such an extent that atomic power became a defining feature of 1950s America and a double-edged symbol both of prosperity and of unease. As Jonathan Hogg and others have demonstrated, there was no lack of debate or discussion about the atomic threat from 1945 onwards in Britain, but its employment as a subject for popular entertainment was sparing in comparison to the US (2016: 45).

Comparisons with Hollywood are, of course, unfair: post-war Britain was beset by economic crisis, with rationing not abolished until 1954. The 1956 Suez crisis, which capsized Anthony Eden's career and Britain's international reputation, only confirmed the country's downward trajectory from world-bestriding power to exhausted, overstretched debtor. Its moral authority, too, so unassailable during and immediately after World War II, was badly dented by the double-dealing involved in Eden's agreement to a ruse with Israel and France over the Suez action and his failure to keep President Eisenhower informed about British plans in the Middle East. This culture of secrecy might go some way towards explaining why, when the *Quatermass* TV dramas and feature films began to appear in the mid-50s, their narratives tended to feature a strong critique of the British people's deference, both to government and to scientists.[5]

It might account, also, for the ascendancy of scientific patriarchs like Bernard in *The Damned* (and like Professor Quatermass himself, whose first feature film incarnation in *The Quatermass Xperiment* is decidedly more hubristic and unsympathetic than he later became). When Bernard tells the children from his screen-pulpit, 'You will be told everything in time, each new thing as you are able to understand it and not before', he's being both a protective father-figure and a mandarin practising deceit in the cause of what he believes is a greater good — not unlike the British state where nuclear (and other) matters were concerned.

Shaw identifies the Boulting brothers' *Seven Days to Noon* (1950) as an early, standout example of a film that tackled the ethics of the nuclear question head-on, by letting a government scientist loose with an atomic 'suitcase bomb' on the streets of London. The film may also mark the beginning of the surreal effects that the nuclear threat has come to exert on morality and logic, for Professor Willingdon appears ready to kill thousands and obliterate the capital in order to bring the world to its senses about the nuclear weapons that he has helped to develop. 'We placed this burden on his shoulders, and left him alone to deal with it,' laments his clergyman friend; something about the world of nuclear weapons can warp a person's moral compass, as though the very subject is radioactive if dwelled upon for long enough. This notion started circulating early, to judge by a *Daily Mail* 'Atomic Age Column' in August 1945, which, says Hogg, introduced readers 'to the idea that common sense is disintegrating in the atomic age' (2016: 61).

Idealism, however, is praiseworthy if not allowed to buckle into such absurdist shapes: in *The Burning Glass* (1954), a stage play by Charles Morgan subsequently adapted for television (1960), the principled Professor Terriford (there's something Quatermassy about that name) fights to keep his device, which can tap and magnify the power of the sun, from the hands of the government and of Communist spies.

While anxieties about nuclear warfare were getting the earnest treatment in dramas such as JB Priestley's *Doomsday for Dyson* (adapted for television in 1958) and Marghanita Laski's *The Offshore Island* (ditto in 1959), a more obscure conception of the nuclear threat as a kind of absurdist contamination also rumbles through the 1950s, cropping up in TV dramas such as *I Can Destroy the Sun* (1958), written by

Hammer's Jimmy Sangster, in which a man threatens to destroy the planets unless the H-bomb is banned. It reaches its height in the unhinged title character of Kubrick's *Dr Strangelove* (1964); it's also abundantly present in *The Damned*, not least in the logic Bernard uses to justify raising the children in isolation and killing anyone who discovers his secret — and it contaminates the notion of heroism, when Simon's determination to free the children, even after he realises that they are lethally radioactive to anyone they come into contact with, begins to seem absurd.

Bunker mentality

> '*Quatermass 2* was about those terrible places that appear in the landscape with nobody knowing what they are, but everybody mutely obeying those "Keep Out" signs.' Nigel Kneale, interview by Robert Muller, 'Quatermass Speaking!' *Daily Mail*, 2 January 1959

The Edgehill Establishment, Bernard's secret facility, would have been a familiar sight to most people in Great Britain by the early 1960s. Along with the development of weapons came the building or expansion of government research facilities and related establishments, all located away from major population centres and shrouded in varying degrees of secrecy: the Chemical Defence Experimental Establishment at Porton Down (opened in 1916 but dedicated after 1945 to research into nerve agents); the Windscale nuclear reactors in Cumbria (which came online in 1951 and 1952), providing plutonium for the UK's nuclear weapons programme; and the Atomic Weapons Research Establishment, which took over the site of RAF Aldermaston in 1950 (and also conducted tests at another off-limits facility, Orford Ness on the Suffolk coast).

Such 'secret establishments' became a regular feature of science fiction from the late 1950s onwards, embodying the growing public distrust in the government's defence programme and anxieties about safety. These concerns were justified by incidents such as the death of an airman during a nerve-gas experiment at Porton Down in 1953, a serious fire at Calder Hall in 1956 and the Windscale fire in 1957. Some of the 'alien facility' scenes in both the BBC serial and Hammer's film of *Quatermass 2* were shot at Shell Haven oil refinery near Stanford-le-Hope, one of dozens of new industrial sites adding to the tally of sinister modern excrescences on the English landscape.

It's easy to forget today, but the phrase 'Like something out of *Quatermass*', was a staple of British conversation in the late 1950s. Kneale's creation became a byword in the press, not just for the threatening strangeness of modern science but of the secrecy of such establishments, whether government-owned or industry-run: a *Daily Mail* report in May 1956 about a strike in a Coventry tractor plant describes the facility as 'Quatermass-like', with '£4,000,000 worth of push-button machinery' about which the reporter was 'pledged to secrecy' (1956: 1). But another, related category of modern architecture, of particular relevance to *The Damned*, took secrecy to such extremes that the very existence of most of the structures concerned was subject to censorship.

In the late 1940s, the tenor of international relations, strained by events such as the Berlin crisis in 1948, prompted parliament to approve the refurbishment and upgrading of the UK's radar system, particularly along the south and east coasts. The scheme, codenamed ROTOR, entered its construction phase in 1951 with the building of several new underground facilities. One of the first to be completed — and, historian Nick McCamley claims, 'probably the most spectacular' (2007: 106) — was a Chain Early Warning station on Portland Bill, 60 feet below the surface. By the time Losey and his film crew arrived, it was no longer operational: changing priorities led to the decommissioning of most of the ROTOR stations, and the Portland site was closed in 1958. But it was still there, a stand-in for the fictional underground facility that Richard MacDonald designed and Hammer built at Bray Studios. It's somehow typical of the absurd universe of *The Damned*, though, that Bernard's project has literally turned the principle of civil defence inside out: the radioactive threat is *inside* the bunker.

Imagining the end

'*When* the time comes,' Bernard intones, not '*If* the time comes'... and the public consensus seemed to be that the time *would* come. George Orwell began his 1945 essay 'You and the Atomic Bomb' by considering 'how likely we all are to be blown to pieces by it within the next five years...' (1945: 6), and this sentiment only intensified in the next two decades: Hogg cites a childhood reminiscence by the poet Liz Lochhead about the air of impending doom at the time of the Cuban Missile Crisis: 'On a placard outside the newsagents, black block capitals spelled WAR INEVITABLE. Even the newsreaders on television looked scared...' (2016: 123). Human nature has shown itself to be obsessed, over the centuries, with imagining mass-scale calamity, and the mid-twentieth century provided a new agent for such a catastrophe. Christoph Laucht draws attention to an article in a 1950 issue of *Picture Post* which envisioned a thermonuclear attack on London using diagrams with concentric circles showing the projected range of devastation (2014: 88). This obsession often has a death-wish kind of edge to it; Kim Newman is not alone in detecting, in many apocalyptic scenarios, 'a half-wished for descent into dog-eat-dog barbarity and the extermination of all the boring people in the world' (1999: 19).

British cinema as far back as 1936 had imagined the UK's cities laid waste by warfare, in the unnervingly prescient HG Wells adaptation *Things to Come*; by the 1950s, a whole range of new fiction took as its starting point a nuclear conflict, as though it were a *fait accompli*. Among the most notable were William Golding's *Lord of the Flies* (1954), John Wyndham's *The Chrysalids* (1955), and Neville Shute's *On the Beach* (1957). In cinema, stories that presented the Third World War as a brief prologue to the main story constituted a genre in itself, from *The World, The Flesh and The Devil* (1959) to *The Last Woman on Earth* (1960). Holding up the absurdist strand was Spike Milligan and John Antrobus' *The Bed Sitting Room*, first performed as a one-act play in 1962, set in a devastated London, nine months after the 'Nuclear Misunderstanding', aka World War III, which lasted for two minutes and twenty-eight seconds, 'including the signing of the peace treaty'.

British artists, too, articulated the atmosphere of atomic-age dread and anxiety in their work: Catherine Jolivette's edited collection of essays, *British Art in the Nuclear Age* (2014), maps some of the more salient features of this movement. There was John Bratby, whose reputation rests on his use of realism and the domestic, but who produced in 1956 a series of canvases that imagined the effects of atomic radiation on the human form, including his own (2014: 157). Then there were landscape artists such as Peter Lanyon, Graham Sutherland and Alan Reynolds, all of whom created work that expressed an unease about landscape and humanity's place in it and effects upon it (2014: 137). *The Damned* has that unease in spades, from its opening shot (presenting a kind of metamorphic, hybrid landscape in which Frink/Freya's art is not always distinguishable from the geological features of the clifftop) to its climax deep inside a landscape co-opted by the military and quarried by the establishment for its own self-aggrandising architecture. Bernard's insistence that the coming conflagration 'will melt those stones' has a trace of the death wish Newman identifies, but also implies that art itself will not survive the apocalypse.

The Damned inhabits an historical moment between the wane of public deference towards the government concerning nuclear weapons (marked by the founding of the Campaign for Nuclear Disarmament (CND) and the beginning of the annual Aldermaston Marches in 1957) and the more full-throated protests and bolder visualisations of nuclear war that appeared mid-decade with films like *Dr Strangelove* and the realist horror-show to rule them all, Peter Watkins' *The War Game* (1965). Also of note was the signing of the Limited Test Ban Treaty in 1963, which committed the signatories to ceasing all above-ground tests — and thus drove the most conspicuous and destructive signs of the Cold War underground, both figuratively and literally. What better time for a film about experiments on radioactive children in a secret subterranean complex?

Footnotes

5. Historical context on post-war Britain, Suez, the Cold War and the nuclear state is supported by the following sources: Sandbrook (2006), Shaw (2006), Hogg (2016). See Bibliography.

Chapter 5: Landscape, Seascape, Manscape

> How well he knew this spot! It was one of those geographical points on the surface of the planet that would surely rush into his mind when he came to die, as a concentrated essence of all that life meant! John Cowper Powys, *Weymouth Sands* (1934: 23)

The Damned was Losey's first feature film in CinemaScope, though not, as most sources claim, his debut with the format; his short for Hammer, *A Man on the Beach*, was shot in CinemaScope. Perhaps this previous experience gave Losey the confidence to take such full advantage of the possibilities offered by this ratio in the opening sequence.

The film's opening shot begins with a slow pan from the open sea to the cliffs of Portland Bill, moving to the left and then down and back to the right in an arc, following the ridge as it rises towards the foreground (Losey, remember, was determined that the film's title be *The Brink*). The course it follows also suggests confinement; the vertical motion is limited, as though tracing a slow, constrained descent that can only be achieved in stages.

James Bernard's score immediately establishes a mood quite unlike that of his usual work for Hammer. A spare melody for flutes and alto saxophone falls and rises in seconds and fourths, evoking, suggests David Huckvale, both Wagner's *Tristan and Isolde* and, more significantly for the English coastal setting, Britten's *Peter Grimes*. Huckvale continues: 'The fourths expand into fifths, then sixths and ultimately into sevenths, before returning to fourths, thereby creating an effective musical metaphor for rising and falling waves' (2006: 118).

Seagulls can be heard on the soundtrack, and a few distant birds seen wheeling above the water. The pan continues past a couple of indistinct forms — the first perhaps just a rock, the second a broken-looking knot of something with stubby limbs like the roots of a molar. On it glides, then up, to find a raised slab of stone and, next to it on a stand (the only 'conventional' object thus far), the sculpted head of a horse. Then it comes to rest on a long table, on which another half-formed object —

a human body, partly eroded or blasted away — reclines none too comfortably.

Pulling out from a shot of an artwork in order to set a scene or a mood was becoming part of Losey's repertoire by this time: at the beginning of *Time Without Pity*, the camera begins on a dense composition of painted figures and then fixates on a Goya reproduction; in *Blind Date*, close-ups of paintings punctuate several scenes; and later in *The Damned*, a scene begins with a cryptic painting hanging on Bernard's wall. Some later criticisms of his work as pretentious or mannered might apply in these cases. But in this opening shot, he begins with the wider view and ends on the artwork. It's a highly effective and intriguing opening: is this the aftermath of something? Are those partial forms all that remains of a few hapless victims? And their horse?

The credits — coming up laconically throughout the panning shot — help us out by displaying, when we reach the equine head, Elisabeth Frink's trademark signature (more of whom later). The final credit, as convention dictates, is the director's, and it appears in its own space to the right of the man-sculpture, rather, one could argue, like a caption, before receding (unlike the rest of the credits) into the distance. Bearing in mind that, for his first two British films, Losey was forced to direct under a pseudonym, perhaps one can forgive him this rather self-aggrandising flourish.

The figure in question, according to Susan Felleman, is one of Frink's 'fallen men' (2014: 109), prefiguring the real falling men we see later, but also leaving us to speculate whether Losey is including it as a self-portrait: the charred shell of a winged man brought to earth, or an artist whose battles with the elemental forces of politics and business have reduced him to this. The later desecration of one of Freya's pieces by King would lend itself to a similar interpretation, as we'll see.

(Incidentally, it's worth comparing this opening to that of Losey's first feature, *The Boy with Green Hair*. In the earlier case, a Technicolour montage of landscape scenes show nature verdant and thriving, as a Hollywood chorus sings an arrangement of the song 'Nature Boy'. In the dozen or so years between the two films, something seems to have happened to nature, or to Losey's view of it: from fertile to barren, and from colour to monochrome.)

The Damned

Figure 1: The film's first fallen man. Self-portrait of its director?

The scene cuts from the prone figure in its stark setting to a long shot, from the sea this time, of the seafront at Weymouth. The final lonesome note of the preceding scene is interrupted by a raucous fanfare of bass and drums, as 'Black Leather Rock', a slightly stodgy rock'n'roll pastiche written by James Bernard, kicks in. The shooting script explains: 'The essential characteristic of the promenade at Weymouth is of two contrasting elements — decayed gentility and modern vulgarity.'

Cut to the top of the Jubilee Clock on the Esplanade, festooned with lights, and we're panning again, straight down this time, taking in the head of Queen Victoria (from falling man to fallen Empire), before veering off to the right near ground level, where Simon, freshly arrived, is about to be snared by Joan. He wears a white hat, contrasting with the song and perhaps denoting his 'good guy' status; but one can't help noticing it's a rather unreassuringly floppy sun hat. 'Never seen a clock tower before?' Joan mocks him, before sashaying off out of frame. He follows, hardly fitting the template of the clean-cut hero, intent as he is on picking up 'a cheap little tart' (as he describes her later); but this is only the first of many incongruities.

Cut to the head of a unicorn statue, with an umbrella hanging from the horn. King and his gang are loitering around it; the camera pulls back, then tilts upwards — mirroring the movement of the camera on the Jubilee Clock — towards the monument to George III. An unstable king if ever there was one; and the second King prowling at street level will prove to be volatile as well.

There's an exchange of looks between King and Joan, the first example of the surveillance theme that occurs throughout, and she leads Simon away from the Esplanade. Cut back to King and co., shot from below, suggesting a certain predatory dominance. But then: 'Forward into battle dear chaps,' says King, adopting a plummy accent. The next shot brings them down a peg or two, by viewing their manoeuvres from the top of the royal monument behind them and following their parodic march away from the seafront as they disrupt traffic and taunt a policeman. This is sport, we're led to conclude, or at least something semi-serious, a pastiche of the military methods that built the now-crumbling Empire. The next scene plays with that seriousness, to great and influential effect.

Figure 2: King and his troops on the Esplanade

Already we've travelled from the windswept existential crags to the gaudy but run-down trappings of a troubled society at leisure, from the 'timeless' and unmeasured to the 'temporal' and regulated. And to accompany them, two contrasting styles of music, and two traditions of representing the human form: Frink's eroded figures, and then the nineteenth-century head of Victoria. That's not to overlook the animal form as well: Frink's rather savage-looking horse suggesting nature red in tooth and claw, contrasted with the glossy unicorn on the Esplanade. The place of art in the modern world is one of the sub-themes of the film, and at the outset, it establishes a polar opposition between the unadorned 'integrity' of the austere modernist artwork (soon to be personified by its creator, Freya Neilson) and the fading kitsch of the Jubilee Clock and the George III monument. The lack of integrity of the latter is immediately emphasised when Joan stops beneath the clock before luring Simon into being mugged.

The Brink

Losey chose Weymouth and Portland Bill as the locations partly because of his love of the Dorset of Thomas Hardy (whose 1897 novel *The Well-Beloved* is set on the Isle of Portland, and even features a chapter entitled 'On the Brink') and John Cowper Powys (whose *Weymouth Sands* begins at the same spot on the Esplanade). Perhaps he also knew of J Meade Falkner's smuggling adventure *Moonfleet* (1898), set near Chesil Beach and filmed in Hollywood by Fritz Lang in 1955 (co-starring, coincidentally, Viveca Lindfors). With his art-world connections he would surely have been acquainted with the work of John Piper (1903-1992), whose distinctive landscapes included a series of ascetic renditions of Portland (reproduced in *The Ambassador* magazine in 1954, for example). Losey's treatment of the island's rugged landscape is quite Piperesque, and closer to the bleak, untethered existentialism of Antonioni or Bergman than the more rooted literature of Hardy and Powys (and indeed, he made his next film, *Eva*, with the Hakim Brothers, who had just produced Antonioni's *L'Eclisse*).

Losey referred to Portland Bill in his interview with Ciment as 'a place where the British were developing germ warfare and also undersea warfare' (1985: 199) — not quite accurate, as others have pointed out. True, the Whitehead Torpedo Works operated for many years at nearby Ferrybridge (my great-great uncle was manager of works there), and the Navy would often test torpedoes in the bay; but as far as germ warfare is concerned, Losey may have been thinking of Porton Down in Wiltshire. This is a far from isolated example of the contested territory represented by names (see 'Appendix').

The area does have resonances with the themes of *The Damned*, however, beyond the presence of the ROTOR facility I mentioned in Chapter 4. One of them is geological: the presence of shale in the local cliffs gave rise, in the 1850s, to the 'burning cliff' phenomenon, when parts of it would burst spontaneously into flame.

The London and Sporting Chronicle carried one such story in December 1849 under the headline 'Discovery of New Light' — ironically, given the title of the film's source novel — and added that 'a company has lately been formed for converting it into an oil, which burns with remarkable brightness'.[6] Which almost sounds like the beginning of a *Quatermass* plot.

A second point to note is that the Isle of Portland is the source of Portland stone, which for centuries has been quarried there and used in the construction of some of the British Empire's signature buildings, including St Paul's Cathedral, the Palace of Westminster and Buckingham Palace — not to mention the hefty pedestal supporting the King's statue on Weymouth esplanade.[7] So the binary opposition of the opening credits isn't so simple: the rocky outcrops in that initial pan are the 'raw' state of the same material that King leans against on the seafront; material that can be used both to buttress and glorify the established order, and to embody the dissenting view of the artist.

A third: the theme of contagion even has a local relevance. According to most histories, the Black Death first came to British shores in 1348 at Melcombe Regis — now part of the town of Weymouth. A plaque on Custom House Quay now proudly records the supposition.[8]

The coast as a geographical feature has often been used in cinema as a transitional, transformational place, as a liminal space, and as a setting for ruminations on mortality, faith and survival. Its use in science fiction and fantasy film takes in *The Seventh Seal* and *On the Beach* (both 1960), *Planet of the Apes* (1968) and countless 'creature features' in which the monster emerges from the sea to menace humanity. In British cinema and television, there are often notes of vulnerability being sounded when the coast appears — not unnaturally for an island nation so recently threatened with invasion. It's also a good spot for epiphanies, breakdowns and hauntings: from the Norfolk coast in the BBC's MR James adaptations *Whistle And I'll Come To You* (1968) and *A Warning To The Curious* (1972) to the Scottish island in Robin Hardy's *The Wicker Man* (1973). In Hammer's earlier science fiction film, *Four-Sided Triangle*, the cloned heroine begins to suffer a mental collapse while on a beach (near Weymouth, in fact), and the studio's cycle of *Psycho*-inspired 'psychological thrillers' that began around 1962 made return visits to the coast for this kind of metaphorical effect: the Camargue-set *Maniac* (1963) (billing partner to *The Damned* in the UK) makes extensive visual use of the local coastline, and *Paranoiac* (1963) even has a strikingly similar opening shot, a pan across the rugged Dorset coastline (the Isle of Purbeck, just east of Portland), all the more reminiscent of *The Damned* because Arthur Grant was the cinematographer for both films. Not only that, but *Paranoiac* notably stars Oliver Reed as another unstable youth — one who has decisively gone *over* the brink.

Sometimes the coast has more practical applications: at the climax of *Day of the Triffids* (1962), the alien plant-creatures are found to dissolve in salt water. These latter two suggest an atavistic link between the sea and evolution; and in *The Damned*, Bernard, in his final scene with Freya (while standing on the edge of a clifftop), speaks of his project in evolutionary terms:

> Life has the power to change... To survive the destruction that is inevitably coming, we need a new kind of man. An accident gave us these nine precious children — the only human beings who have a chance to live in the conditions which must inevitably exist when the time comes.

The irony of the coastal setting and the associations it evokes is that the immediate threat to the protagonists comes not from beyond this geographical boundary, but from *within* it.

Coast and carnival

The second coast — the 'seaside', the resort, teeming with humanity and hilarity, pier shows, McGill postcards, donkey rides — is, in *The Damned*, rather overlooked. Compared to something like Tony Richardson's film of John Osborne's play *The Entertainer* or Michael Winner's *The System*, the seaside setting is more an establishing shot than an environment in itself (unlike the opening coastal shot). Losey, never one for letting his hair down, seems uninterested in the British at play — or rather, it's the play of King's gang that interests him, as we'll see in the next chapter.

But the possibilities of the British seaside resort, exploited as they have been throughout cinema history — from George Arthur Smith's *A Visit to the Seaside* (1908) to the *Carry On* series and beyond — are realised, to an extent, in *The Damned*. As Jez Conolly points out, citing Mikhail Bakhtin's famous study of Rabelais, the seaside presents an arena for the 'carnivalesque', or 'a space in which conventional hierarchies of authority may be overturned' (2008: 11). He quotes Bakhtin's explanation of how the medieval notion of carnival operates:

> What is suspended first of all is hierarchical structure and all the forms of terror, reverence, piety, and etiquette connected with it — that is, everything resulting from sociohierarchical inequality or any other form of inequality among people (including age). (2008: 17)

King's gang, as they mock-march into the traffic, are enacting that spirit of carnival, thumbing their noses at the law and confounding any expectations of deference to their 'superiors'. But it's the work of the film to show how hierarchical structure, even in its weakened condition post-Empire and post-Suez, reasserts itself through violence and the tools of the state. Carnival, after all, is sanctioned by the powers that be because it's a *temporary* suspension of social norms. Long after King has come to a watery end, the Jubilee Clock and the George III monument will still be standing.

The next scene is short, sharp and, compared to what came before, a shock, and it completes the first section of the film. In a residential street, King marches at the head of his troops, brolly shouldered like a rifle, the company (except for Sid) still whistling 'Black Leather', in a parody of the 'Colonel Bogey' theme from the fairly recently released *The Bridge on the River Kwai* (1957). The camera, in front of them, dollies backwards and rounds a corner, anticipating the gang's route; one could say the camera is complicit, or at least in on the game.

Simon and Joan follow, arm in arm. And here's another incongruity: they walk only a few yards behind her brother's cronies; she sings along to 'Black Leather', and smiles warmly at him; he smiles back, unaware that he's a mark and unconcerned about the whistling bikers directly in front of them. Simon looks as though he's happily joined their carnivalesque parade. Clearly, Val-Guest-style realism — indeed, British-cinema-style realism — is not the operative mode. This is a Brechtian mugging if ever there was one, stated in a rapid series of broad gestures.[9]

The gang ducks behind a rough stone wall that occupies the far left of the frame; the camera movement slows, rises a little to accommodate Simon's approach. King's head skulks in the bottom corner; he spreads his leather-gloved hands over the white surface of the end of the wall, in a gesture that resounds in several ways later on (see 'Appendix'). Here, it signifies the impending downfall of the white-hat-wearing 'good guy'.

The handle of King's brolly, wielded by an offscreen Sid, hooks Simon's neck — a cartoonish manoeuvre perhaps inspired by the gang's watching a Looney Tunes short before *Bridge on the River Kwai* — and down he goes, the first of the film's flesh-and-blood falling men. Then a series of rapid cuts as members of the gang take turns punching him. Punching the camera, rather, which is no longer an honorary gang member but, taking Simon's point of view for a few frames, is on the receiving end of the violence. By implication, we the viewers are also being assaulted. Later, other watchers will also come under attack.

The larks of the previous scene have turned vicious, but King carries on whistling. Ted (Tom Kempinski), crouching next to Simon, goes through his pockets and passes one or two items up to King. The camera watches King from below as he takes a cigarette from Simon's packet and glances at his passport then flings it down at him.

'Are you happy in your work, Joanie?' asks Sid the Ambivalent Biker. If Simon is the film's 'uncommitted liberal', Sid is its uncommitted thug. Joan looks as unhappy as he does. They're the gang's conscience, it seems, though not a very highly developed one at first.

Cut to a shot just above pavement level: Simon lies bruised and unconscious on the ground. King's brolly taps him several times. King adopts his army voice: 'By the left... quick march,' and a thicket of black-trousered legs marches away into the background. Simon's white hat lies crumpled next to him — the last time we see it. On *his* head, anyway.

There's no definitive proof that Stanley Kubrick was influenced by this scene in his shooting of the home invasion scene in *A Clockwork Orange* (1971); the similarities

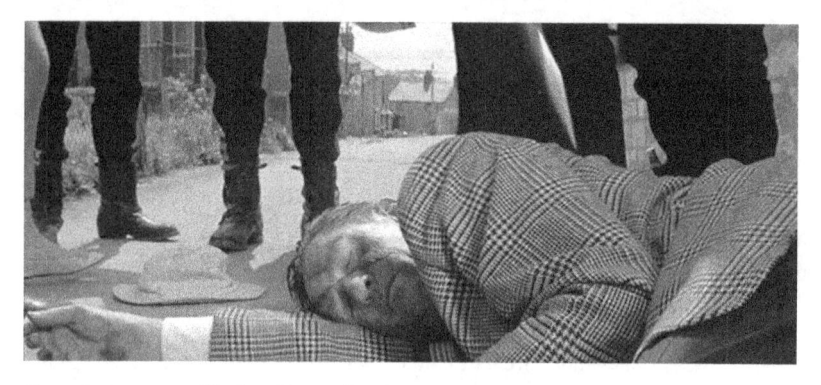

Figure 3: A prone and hatless Simon after the mugging

— the delinquent gang, the use of an umbrella, the combination of violence and popular song (*Singin' in the Rain* (1952), in Kubrick's case) — certainly suggest it, though Losey, speaking to Ciment, pronounced himself dubious (1985: 200). At the very least, *The Damned* anticipates Kubrick's view of violence as something enacted at the establishment level as well as the personal level, often more ruthlessly and less transparently.

The final shot completes a kind of circle that began with the opening credits: the camera holds for a few seconds on the figure of a fallen man, like Frink's sculpture come to life. There are many circular motions in *The Damned*; this is a wide orbit compared to the tightening patterns to come.

Footnotes

6. Quoted at www.scottishshale.co.uk/GazBeyond/BSEnglandShale/BSES_Works/WeymouthOilWorks.html (accessed 30-4-17).
7. See the entry for the monument on the Historic England website: www.historicengland.org.uk/listing/the-list/list-entry/1365879 (accessed 30-4-17).
8. For details and images, see 'Dorset's plague port', *Dorset Life*, November 2009: www.dorsetlife.co.uk/2009/11/dorset%E2%80%99s-plague-port/ (accessed 30-4-17).
9. We can add one more incongruity to the pile, this time a literal one: the street, Albert Terrace, is not in Weymouth at all, but in Fortuneswell on the Isle of Portland – over five miles from where Joan picked up Simon.

Chapter 6: Damned Kids

Look for a parent in *The Damned*'s cast of characters — a natural, biological one — and you'll come up short. King's gang, if not actually orphans, are given no mothers or fathers to rail against; neither Bernard nor Freya, we assume, have children; if Hammond or any of the other military men have families, we never know of them. The children themselves, of course, are orphans, or at least motherless, and there is also an absence of the 'domestic', in the sense that we never see a 'home' in the conventional sense. Yet parenthood, childhood, generative power, are strong themes in the film, as they are in the *Quatermass* films and *X the Unknown* (although the earlier films tended to show violations of the domestic as an indication of the threat to normality and way of life).

So who, exactly, are 'The Damned'? The children are the obvious answer: the novel's title makes them the subject, and the film flips their polarity from blessed to not-so-blessed. The US poster for *These are the Damned* places one of the children, spookily rendered, in the centre, and uses the tagline:

CHILDREN OF ICE AND DARKNESS! THEY ARE THE LURKING UNSEEN EVIL YOU DARE NOT FACE ALONE!

Case closed, says the promotion. The film's British poster, however, picks out King and his gang as the subjects of the title, and uses a publicity still showing Reed astride a motorcycle, flanked by the others, closing in menacingly on Field. The image was one of a series from a photoshoot by the unit's still photographer, Tom Edwards, under the direction of the poster's designer, John Stockle. As Marcus Hearn notes, '… although the shots bore no resemblance to any scenes from the film they went on to dominate the front-of-house set', and gave punters the impression 'that this was less a science fiction thriller and more a film in the tradition of *The Wild One* (1953).' (2010: 15)

Muddying the water still further is the tagline: 'All of them doomed by the lurking, unseen evil'. So the gang are presented both as the antagonists and as the victims of another antagonist, the 'evil'. But this does preserve, however confusingly, some of Losey's stated intention to show violence enacted at different social levels.

Leather boys

Let's take the bikers first, since they appear first. We've just seen them marching up the high street into 'battle', whistling the 'Black Leather' chorus. On the one hand, they're indulging in the carnivalesque behaviour mentioned in the last chapter, merrily disrupting the hierarchical order; but one could argue that this is a *parody* of carnival enacted by a new, cynical generation. King and his 'chaps' muck about in kids' cowboy hats, and later prance about on the beach playing (of course) 'King of the Castle', but they're outsiders, not part of the social contract that governs the smooth running of the seaside and its (sanctioned) carnival aspects.

Their status is inadvertently reinforced by the conditions of filming: the logistics of shooting in a busy street populated by real people rather than hundreds of costly extras creates a division between actors and the public. The locals, rather awkwardly, are onlookers in this and several other Weymouth scenes, reacting to these 'outsiders' as they cause genuine disruption to the town's routine.

The gang, of course, represents a mirror-image for Bernard and his soldiers, and Losey has far greater sympathy for King and company — 'because they don't know what they're doing,' he told Michel Ciment. 'And they have still some of the innocence of kids. And they are not responsible for what they are' (1985: 202).

But 'what they are' is an open question. Major Holland calls them 'Teddy Boys', but that may be an indication of how out of touch he is: their clothes are all wrong for Teddy Boys, and by 1960 the Teddy Boy subculture was on the wane (Stanley Cohen describes how, even before the end of the previous decade, 'Teddy Boy suits were already being sold at jumble sales' (2002: 156)). Losey himself had a characteristically class-oriented explanation for using the Teddy Boy label (having been in his early fifties at the time of *The Damned*, perhaps he can be excused for being a little behind the times himself):

> The Victorian-Edwardian seaside resort was absolutely ideal ... it was obviously a kind of place for the Teddy boys, whose name is a diminutive for Edward because they affected Edwardian dress... This past was over but it was pretty degenerate too. And the Teddy boys were a result of that degeneration ... they were the sons

of the servants and the general workmen that maintained these resorts for the rich when they were still there. So now you have the children of the working class trying to recapture some kind of power out of past elegance by wearing Edwardian clothes. (1985: 200)

Losey's commentary is interesting but imprecise. The era's new 'folk devils' were the Mods and the Rockers, and what the gang appears to be is a bunch of Rockers led by a Mod — an appropriately unlikely setup for a film that wears its incongruities so much on its sleeve. However, to be fair, Cohen dates the emergence of a public sense of division between the Mods and the Rockers at 1962-63, at least a year after *The Damned* was made, but roughly contemporary with its delayed UK release in 1963. So perhaps this wasn't so incongruous at the time of shooting (2002: 156).

The post-war phenomenon of the Teddy Boys, the Mods, the Rockers and their successors is inextricable from the climate of atomic terror, according to many commentators. The psychologist DW Winnicott suggested that the shadow of nuclear warfare was responsible for creating a permanent state of adolescence (1984: 151). Jeff Nuttall, whose influential manifesto-cum-memoir *Bomb Culture* charted the landscape that had to be negotiated by the younger generations in the West, described the psychological fallout from the politics of their elders:

It was impossible to live with the bomb and the cold war and retain the sympathetic faculties. The situation remained, so sensitivity had to go. The mods and the rockers were not only the next step in the excitement game, they were the extended, tawdry funeral of compassion. It was the only way the growing mind could deal with the constant probability of unprecedented pain and horror which the squares took such trouble to preserve. (1968: 37)

But taking another look at King and his gang, and with a sociological study like Cohen's *Folk Devils and Moral Panics* to hand, one can argue that their cross-tribe makeup, while not chiming with one's sense of realism (which Losey's films often don't), gets at something more symbolic of a deeper order (which Losey's films often do). In Cohen's dissection of media assumptions about the Mods and Rockers, he suggests that, by 1963, '[t]he Rockers were left out of the race: they were unfashionable and unglamorous just because they appeared to be more class-bound... The Mods, on the other hand, made all the running... This was the Mod era...' (2002: 156). Naturally enough, then, the Mod leads the Rockers.

Despite his comments about class and youth revolt and his evident sympathy for their position, Losey doesn't dwell on the sociology of the gang or the circumstances of their delinquency; of the seven members, we only come to know three as individuals. British films about delinquent youth had a lineage of their own, stretching back at least to the borstal drama *Boys in Brown* (1949), and acquiring more of the trappings of youth culture by the time of Lewis Gilbert's *Cosh Boy* (1953) and Basil Dearden's *Violent Playground* (1958), but *The Damned* is a red herring in such company. It lacks the hinterland of moral guardians, enforcers and concerned elders, or even a real sense that King's bikers are a 'problem' to be addressed, and therein, perhaps, lay some of the BBFC's concerns about the tone of the script. Bernard's lament that 'The age of senseless violence has caught up with us too' is virtually all he has to say on the youth delinquency problem, and the line is principally there for the purposes of irony.

Indeed, later on, when Hammond interrogates Ted from the gang, there's little sense of a moral high ground from which Hammond is speaking, even though he clearly looks down on them: by the end of the interrogation, it's as though the soldier and the biker have come to an understanding that both are members of a 'subculture', each with its own conventions. For Losey, there's no biker gang without the military gang; their existence within the same social order is the whole point. This was a recurring idea in his films: parallel worlds operating at different social levels. In *M*, law enforcement and the criminal underworld are led into co-operating by a common interest in catching the child-murderer; and in the confined world of *The Criminal*, the warders and the inmates are mutually complicit in a number of ways.

Losey reinforces this idea by suggesting visual similarities between the two leaders: King and Bernard both dress in semi-formal check jackets, a style that contrasts with those under their command, and both carry umbrellas. The parallels between them go even deeper, since both are engaged in repressive actions: Bernard keeping the children confined underground, King ruling his sister possessively — to the extent, we are told, of locking her in a cupboard for a week when a man showed interest in her (not to mention his own sexual self-repression). The shooting script shows how explicitly planned this mirroring was: the interrogation scene contains the following direction:

> HOLLAND's swagger stick comes up in an almost involuntary gesture so that the point of it is now in the same position in front of TED's face as King's dagger was when he threatened Joan.

For all his thuggish bearing, though, King, and by extension his gang, are clearly given some of the attributes of the child: besides their play-acting on the Esplanade, his taunts of 'Simple Simon' are playground-level stuff, and his reaction to Joan's suggestion that he hasn't yet lost his virginity suggests a kind of adolescent shame. Still, King and co aren't children, even if they seem to have been stranded in a state of arrested development just shy of adulthood. To find any actual children in *The Damned*, you have to go underground.

The child in time

Bernard's children — well-spoken, precocious, innocent but deadly — have a lineage that is particularly British in origin. They also share with a handful of contemporary films the distinction of introducing something sinister into the cultural iconography of the child.

Figure 4: Bernard addresses the children

British cinema in the 1940s began to specialise in a certain representation of the child that resonated with the concerns of a country at war: at first, there were the straightforward 'why we fight' messages that presented children as the future of the nation and used them as symbols both of potential and of vulnerability. In Humphrey Jennings' short propaganda film *Words for Battle* (1941), children frolic in a pastoral scene while Laurence Olivier recites lines from Blake's *Jerusalem* (Losey made a short film on a parallel theme, *A Child Went Forth*, in the same year); and in his *Diary for Timothy* (1945), advice to a new-born infant is intercut with more Blakean imagery, and with scenes of Britain at war. The tone struck by Michael Redgrave's narration — paternalistic, sober, gentle but cautioning, uttering warnings like 'You're in danger, Tim...' — isn't a million miles from some of Bernard's pronouncements to the children ('Big people are dangerous to you'). The same impulse is at work in both cases: to safeguard the future of (British) humanity by careful moral instruction. But Timothy's mother hasn't been killed by radiation, and the Cold War has yet to begin. Redgrave's narrator — effectively the voice of the British state — has the kind of unimpeachable authority that Bernard strives after, and the newborn Timothy, unlike the captive children of *The Damned*, can't answer back.

The figure of the child, in these late-war and post-war British films, was a tabula rasa onto which a range of ideas could be projected. Most straightforward was the 'preying on the innocent' idea: in *The Third Man* (1949), for example, Holly Martins (Joseph Cotten) is forced to acknowledge the criminal depths to which his friend Harry Lime (Orson Welles) has sunk when he is shown a ward full of child-victims of the diluted penicillin Lime has been peddling. Vicissitudes of wartime such as orphanhood, poverty, evacuation and sudden reversals of fortune, meanwhile, found their cinematic reflection in the handful of post-war Dickens adaptations, including David Lean's *Great Expectations* (1946) and *Oliver Twist* (1948), and Cavalcanti's *The Life and Adventures of Nicholas Nickleby* (1947). Children could symbolise good-natured, anarchic resilience in the face of hardship, especially when banded together in groups, as they were in the early Ealing comedy *Hue and Cry* (1947); or they could be pampered, pale, trusting creatures betrayed by grownups, such as Philippe (Bobby Henrey) who hero-worships his father's butler, Baines (Ralph Richardson) only to be disillusioned in Carol Reed's *The Fallen Idol* (1948).

Occasionally, a film would attempt something more unusual. In *The Rocking-Horse Winner* (1949), based on a short story by DH Lawrence, little Paul Grahame (John Howard Davies), the sensitive son of a family in debt, discovers that he can pick the winners of horse races while he rides his rocking horse. The fable-like story shows Paul as a forebear of the *Damned* children: an outsider on the one hand by dint of his gift for prophecy, but also a captive, trapped by his desire to help his wastrel parents out of debt and haunted by the family house that he imagines talking to him about the need for more money. The strain of riding himself into a trance in order to pick the right horses finally finishes him off, a victim of his parents' selfishness and his own sense of filial duty. Ultimately, and not unusually, the film blames the mother for the fate of the child.

Where nuclear matters are concerned, in public discourse post-1945, the child again becomes a receptacle for anxieties about the future. Hogg produces several examples that chime with our themes here, such as the 25 August 1945 cover of the *Picture Post* which carried a photograph of a young boy standing alone on a beach (the coast again) and looking out to sea, with the headline 'Man enters the atom age: Dawn or Dusk?' (2016: 60), and an article in the *Guardian* in October 1963 about the discovery of increased levels of 'radio-strontium' in the bones of children (2016: 119).

With *Village of the Damned* (1960), adapted from John Wyndham's 1957 novel *The Midwich Cuckoos*, a new breed of child emerged: angelic in appearance, monstrous in nature, and at least half-alien. Born to every woman of child-bearing age in the village of Midwich and growing rapidly, these children soon develop beyond mere precociousness and into a freakishly supernatural group of beings who can read, and control, people's minds. The scientist-figure — of course there is one — is Professor Zellaby (George Sanders), 'father' of one of the cuckoos, who persuades the authorities to let him sequester the children in a schoolhouse and try both to educate and to study them (prefiguring the confinement of the nine in *The Damned*). He waxes optimistic: 'Who's to say that these children are not the answer [...] to wars, to disease, to human want and misery and all of the problems we've been unable to cope with'. But his idealism is, as so often in such scenarios, shown to be misguided. After the children cause several deaths in the village and the true scale of their threatening abilities becomes apparent, Zellaby himself brings about their end, and his own, during a lesson on — of all things — atomic energy. The film ends with the burning schoolhouse; like the alien facility in *Quatermass 2* with its growing alien life-forms, the threat is simply too great, or too complex, to do anything but destroy it.

The sort-of sequel, *Children of the Damned* (1964), takes a more ambivalent approach to the children's essential natures. These hive-minded minors are victims of an uncomprehending establishment, literally besieged (inside a derelict church) and, although still inclined to murder and maim, not the ruthless alien creatures of the first film. They're not alien at all, it transpires, but — according to a scientist who examines their blood cells — a more advanced form of human (much as Bernard speaks of the children as the next stage in human evolution). Moreover, their otherworldliness has a messianic aspect, since they were all, we are told, conceived without a father. After a Cold-War-style escalation of hostilities from the authorities, the discovery that the children are human leads the head of the military to call off a planned all-out assault, only for an accident to precipitate the destruction of the church and the children.

In the US, a poster for *These are the Damned* featured an image of a child with uncanny staring eyes — a surely deliberate callback to the one used to promote *Village of the Damned*. The two sets of children are not all that similar, beyond their clipped speech patterns: Bernard's wards are not alien progeny, and they lack the arresting eyes, the (in the film at any rate) uniformly pale blond hair, the telepathy and the affectless manner of the 'cuckoos'. The nine children are a hybrid of the Dickensian vulnerable and the Wyndhamesque monstrous, both victim and agent of harm; in this sense, they share a relationship with the children in another British film of the same period, Jack Clayton's *The Innocents* (1961), based on Henry James' novella *The Turn of the Screw* (1898). Clayton was careful to preserve a sense of ambivalence about the film's two precocious siblings, Miles and Flora, effectively orphaned by their absentee father (Michael Redgrave). Their highly-strung governess, Miss Giddens (Deborah Kerr), becomes convinced that the children are in the grip of an evil possession by two dead servants; we are left to wonder whether her own instability has driven her to this conclusion. But the poise and maturity of the pair, especially of Miles, is presented as uncanny and unnatural; and while they seem wise beyond their years, they lack, as King and his gang do (and to a degree the bunker-bound children), the 'sympathetic faculties' that Nuttall describes.

There's also a hint of a shared language concerning the threat posed by the children: Miss Giddens expresses her feelings about the 'wickedness' that she senses in Miles, after discovering that he has been expelled from his boarding school, in terms of a sickness that may be catchable: she likes a boy with spirit, she says, 'but not to the degree to... contaminate.' She promptly amends this with 'To corrupt', a verb much more in keeping with the character's repressed Christian upbringing, but 'contaminate' is a striking word to light upon first. Her phrases are lifted verbatim from James' story, but their survival in the screenplay suggests an awareness of its atomic-age associations.

The Innocents, as Christopher Frayling observes in his DVD commentary, is shot through with images and ideas of 'decay from within', something deliberately emphasised by Truman Capote's Southern-Gothic-influenced contributions to the screenplay; in *The Damned*, too, the threat comes from an interior source, or rather from several: on a national level, it's the government rather than a foreign power that has sponsored the secret project; on a geographical level, the children are held inside the landscape; and on a physiological level, their lethal qualities originate in their own bodies and were acquired *in utero*. In both films, then, the minds and bodies of children are 'contaminated', 'corrupted', by an older generation.

This process is even at work in the children's mannerisms and speech patterns: the Wyndham cuckoos, the Jamesian prodigies and the radioactive pre-teens all display the precociousness that now seems so stilted in films of a certain vintage. But the qualities that signified stoicism and pluck in children who graced wartime dramas such as (to pick an example almost at random) *In Which We Serve* (1942) had become, by the late 1950s, the symptoms of a cold, unnatural and quite possibly alien nature. These freakish specimens often speak like adults, and even their childish pronouncements are delivered with faultless elocution. In *Village of the Damned*, their affectless poise marks them out as otherworldly (though the glowing eyes are also a giveaway); but elsewhere, these mannerisms are attributable at least as much to a shuttered education. In *The Innocents*, the perfectly spoken Miles and Flora are being raised like hothouse flowers (again, very Southern-Gothic); in *The Damned*, the isolated children are more like test subjects, and their speech patterns are roughly what one might expect of children exposed only to Bernard's severe cadences and Captain Gregory's (James Villiers) plummy renditions of great literature (if his reading of Byron's 'Prisoner of Chillon' is anything to go by). Never mind radiation — this is contamination by poetry.

Perhaps the lineage of these children would be incomplete without one further model: the young Joseph Losey. The director, having loudly disdained science fiction as a genre, explained to Milne that his interest in the project arose from the theme of the 'irresponsible use of the new atomic powers put into the hands of the human race' (1968: 32), but as a child he suffered frequent bouts of asthma and was confined to the family home, where he read voraciously and, according to De Rham, was given private tuition while his peers were pursuing a more active, social school career on the 'outside' (1991: 6). Did he see something of his younger self in the children's predicament?

To return to the question at the top of the chapter: Who are 'The Damned'? Clearly, it's the young in general, consigned to an uncertain fate by nuclear proliferation and the Cold War, by the establishment struggling to maintain the vestiges of an empire, and by social attitudes that see them as a problem to be contained. More specifically, one could argue that the young in the film itself are damned by their exile from the domestic. For normality and the nuclear family were not just the thing under threat; as Hogg suggests, in the public discourse of common-sense reassurances, 'domestic tranquility was mobilized against the dark abyss' of Cold War anxiety (2016: 97). No such compensation is available to the young in *The Damned*.

Chapter 7: Creating Woman, Falling Man

The birdhouse — Freya's retreat on the cliffs of Portland Bill — is a space with special properties. It's an artist's habitat, a female space, a shelter on the edge of a brink. Grass grows on the roof, making it almost a part of the landscape, half-cave.

'It's a fabulous place,' says Simon when he and Joan first climb inside. 'You should see it in the fog,' she replies, becoming uncharacteristically lyrical. 'It's wild and weird. Those rocks, dissolving as if into cloud...' Shortly thereafter, they share their first (consensual) kiss; presiding over the scene on a shelf in the background is a thin male figure, arms raised, like a genius loci somehow conducting the proceedings. Characters who visit this space undergo an alteration, as other aspects of themselves are revealed.

In a film devoid of parents, the birdhouse is also the closest thing to a fertile, regenerative place, and all the more of an 'oasis' for its location amidst the austere rock of Portland. The house is alive with Freya's creations and half-finished work. After he and Joan consummate their relationship in Freya's bed, Simon says: 'I've never found this kind of quietness before. It's as if I were no longer afraid of dying.'

Bernard's house — Edgecliff House — stands nearby, a contrast in every way. Further from the edge, regular and unimaginative in shape, furnished inside with modern comforts and featuring a TV camera and monitor in the living room, Edgecliff House is to the birdhouse as the Jubilee Clock is to Freya's sculpture in the opening credits: shiny, contrived and not to be trusted. A few pieces of Freya's art are visible, sitting on a mantelpiece or a shelf; more art hangs framed on the wall.

We first see this room at the end of a transition that takes us from the crags and waters of Portland Bill to this interior via a travelling matte — and not a very convincing one, even for 1961. It delivers a jolt, I think, as all ropey effects do, and unintentionally sets us up for the contrivances and subterfuge being committed by the Edgecliff project.

Bernard's education 'experts' are wrangling with Major Holland (Walter Gotell) and Captain Gregory (James Villiers) about authority and obedience. 'If it was up to you,

you'd turn all these children into beatniks,' says Holland, perhaps thinking of the sculptress at the bottom of the garden.

Women artists were not a common sight in the cinema of the period; in fact, it's hard to think of any that predate Freya in *The Damned* — any who are treated seriously, anyway. The introduction of this worldly, European female artist is the film's biggest alteration from the novel, and is a piece of brilliance on Losey's part. Yes, it risks pretension, and some critics judged that the risk was realised, but its effects on the dynamics and the structure of the film are invigorating.

As we've seen, her sculptures provide an answering force for the kitsch on the Esplanade and the corrupt powers that it represents. The use of Elisabeth Frink's work is crucial to the film's tone and its imagery; Losey conceived the part of Freya with her art in mind, having lately become acquainted with her, and even considered casting her, as Frink recalled in an interview:

> I had to go down to Portland [...] to teach Viveca Lindfors some lessons in how to build up in plaster. To begin with, Joe Losey wanted me to take the part of the sculptress [...] I said 'Would it be a very big part?' and he said 'No no, it'll be quite alright, you'll be there sculpting in the background'. So I said yes I would. And then the part became so complicated and so important, it was quite obvious that I couldn't do it, and didn't want to. (1985)

Elisabeth Frink (1930-1993) was among a new generation of British sculptors who emerged after the Second World War as a group devoted to reflecting the damage to humanity inflicted by the war and the horror of the new age of atomic weaponry. The critic Herbert Read, in the catalogue for an exhibition at the 1952 Venice Biennale called New Aspects of British Sculpture, wrote of this group: 'here are images of flights, frustrated sex, the geometry of fear'.

Among her principal subjects were men (almost never women), birds and horses, and the manner in which she rendered them emphasised vulnerability, struggle, damage. Flight is a common theme, but it's a compromised notion in her sculptures: wings are truncated, clearly inadequate for the task. Frink herself attributed this to seeing so many fighter planes shot down as a child: 'I was obsessed with flight, and aeroplanes crashing, because they crashed all round us' (1992: 20). This imagery thus draws on her own experience of World War II to evoke fears about warfare in general, and 'the next war' in particular. It also suits perfectly the film's theme of falling.[10]

Some of Frink's contemporaries could have supplied the artwork almost as effectively: Bernard Meadows, with pieces such as *Fallen Bird* (1958), was among many sculptors and painters who depicted hybrid or mutated animal forms, including, as Robert Burstow describes them, 'winged creatures... deprived of the power of flight' (2014: 67); Peter Lanyon took a 'metamorphic' approach to landscape painting in a series of works that turned the land inside out to create a subjective account of the terrain and its strata, in ways that resonate with Losey's treatment of Portland Bill. But the choice of Frink is spot-on, not just because of the many pieces of hers that populate the film, but because of the character of Freya that Losey and Jones extrapolate from Frink's work, and from Frink herself. The era produced several British films featuring artists — *The Horse's Mouth* (1958), *The Rebel* (1961), Losey's own *Blind Date* — and often had fun with the inherent pretentiousness of the existential worldview, but no film of the period used art, and the artist, in quite the serious way that *The Damned* does.

Freya herself provides an extra dimension not just to the film but to the other characters. Bernard is not simply a buttoned-down technocrat, but Freya's ex-lover, a fact that at first seems implausible but suggests that Bernard has evolved — or *devolved* — from a more rounded, full-blooded man to the monomaniac we meet in Weymouth.[11] His appreciation of Freya's art, in this light, hints at something redemptive, like the glint of humanity still evident in the mutated Victor Carroon in *The Quatermass Xperiment*: not sufficient to save him from monstrosity, perhaps, but just enough to make him sympathetic. Sid the Ambivalent Biker also gets a humanising and rather touching moment with Freya towards the film's climax.

Freya supplies us with some orientation concerning Simon Wells, about whom we initially may have had our doubts as a suitable hero (picking up a local tart, indeed): their exchange on the hotel verandah, during which Freya watches him intently, establishes Simon as a rebel, though a rather muddled one:

SIMON: I like to listen to people who know what they're talking about. My trouble is I never believe anything they say.

FREYA: Good for you.

SIMON: Think so?

FREYA: Yes, I do.

SIMON: I don't. The people who know all the answers are much happier.

FREYA: Then why aren't you one of them?

SIMON: I just told you, I don't like the answers.

Shortly afterwards, Freya confirms her approval to Bernard: 'I like him because he doesn't like the world. It's a good beginning.' This seems an eloquent assessment, until one tries to make sense of it. A good beginning for what? For making sense of the world? For a friendship with Freya? Her prerogative as a character, though, is to resist the tyranny of (male) meaning, to ask questions, and frequently to unsettle the male characters.

Freya thus represents a threat to the masculinity around her.[12] It's not just that she is independent, opinionated, argumentative; like Frink's, her human forms are all male, and her art brings the weaknesses of man out into the open by showing them falling/fallen, wounded, distressed. The confrontation between her and King is a high point of the film, leaving neither of them unscathed.

It's worth taking a closer look at this scene, which uses the CinemaScope format and the 'pre-design' work of Richard MacDonald to establish a female space and to send an intruding male psyche into a crisis from which it doesn't recover.

King and Freya on the brink

Simon and Joan have just consummated their relationship in Freya's bed and, hearing the approach of an engine and fearing that it's King, have fled from the birdhouse.

The Damned

Figure 5: Freya in the doorway of the birdhouse

The scene begins with a long static shot, from the other side of the room, of the darkened doorway of the birdhouse and the broad sweep of this main entrance space. On the far right is the outline of an equine head, on the far left a human form dimly illuminated. In the foreground, stretched horizontally, is a long, indistinct shape, extending the width of the frame, that looks roughly carved or hollowed out, like a wooden canoe or a hammock (and reminiscent of the 'fallen man' sculpture in the opening credits shot). Farther back and towards the right, another, smaller human figure stands at the window looking out. The three pieces of art frame the lower half of the screen and form a kind of welcoming cradle for Freya, who opens the front door, her figure outlined in the doorway. A little extra light spills into the room from the headlights of her sports car parked outside.

She busies herself with adjusting parts of the room. This is her space; despite the clutter, the impression is of stability, familiarity. Switching on a light discloses a sculpted male form, a helmeted warrior, in the centre of the frame, against the wall between the door and the window.

We've seen this space before, in daylight, when Simon and Joan break in; then, the editing explores parts of the room's interior bit by bit, as a process of discovery that forms a setting for their growing intimacy. But in this second presentation, we see it differently. This single, static shot shows the pieces of artwork arranged in a tableau; despite their rough, ragged aspects, the sculptures are part of a larger whole.

The contrast with the first scene in the classroom is marked: there, the smooth, neutral surfaces, low ceiling and strip lighting, and the long narrow rectangle of blackboard, not to mention the TV screen in the centre of it, emphasised confinement and control; here, the rough stone walls and sculptures suggest not just freedom and creativity but an embrace of chaos and of natural forces. The binary opposition of the opening sequence is restated in these two spaces, but linked, as all oppositions are, even if only by a thread: Freya and Bernard were lovers and still share an affinity, however strained, as hinted at by his appreciation of her graveyard bird.

Cut to Freya in the doorway to the adjoining room, the kitchen/bedroom. Something catches her eye and she looks troubled. A reverse-angle shot of the bedroom shows the remnants of Simon and Joan's presence on the table in the foreground. She steps back into the main room and calls: 'Is anybody there?' Slowly she turns back to the adjoining room. 'I know I'm sloppy,' she says to herself, and pauses before concluding, 'but I'm not that bad.'

We cut to a view of the room from the other side of the bed. In the foreground are its disordered blankets, in a composition very similar to that of the hollowed-out shape in the previous room (and again suggesting a visual rhyme with the 'fallen man' in the opening shot). From one part of the house to the next, the results of creative activity and sexual activity thus occupy the same space in the frame. And with their hollows and folds, both could be described, with a bit of Freudian licence, as vaginal.

Freya picks up the drink glasses and mutters: 'Two of them?' After another pause, she walks over to the bed and, with what seems an amused expression, sits down on it. In the meantime, King has appeared at the doorway. The camera pans left, ostensibly to balance the composition, but it's as though his entry has caused a disturbance. After a brief cut to King in the doorway, with the same setup as the earlier shot of Freya there, we cut back to the 'master' shot. Freya examines the pillows on her bed, and cuffs them, amused, as though she's ruffling the hair of a charming urchin. King takes another step and she turns.

'What can I do for you, sir?' she asks as he approaches. 'Would you mind getting out of my bedroom?' King grasps the bedstead as if for support. A few moments ago,

Freya was troubled by the idea of a presence ('Is anyone there?'); now King, troubled by the idea of absence, looks at the pillows and demands: 'Where's Joanie?' It's his sister's absence of course, but if we carry on taking Freudian licence, the absence is another manifestation of the female space he has wandered into.

After a further exchange, Freya ushers King with mock courtesy back into the main room. The framing is tighter than before: its main elements are King, the warrior sculpture, Freya and the outside doorway. Another brief verbal skirmish leaves King feeling outsmarted. He turns his attention to the warrior. He places his hands — ungloved now, perhaps to signify vulnerability — on either side of the neck, as if about to strangle it. 'I know your kind,' he mutters. 'Smart talking, bad living. People with no morals.'

'Maybe my morals are different from yours,' she says, getting up and walking outside.

'You don't have any!' he snaps, repeating himself, so apparently troubled is he about this further absence, in a house so overwhelmingly female that even its name, 'the birdhouse', suggests it. Left alone, he looks around: cut to two reverse-angle shots (both sparsely composed in contrast to the rest of the scene, and dramatically lit, throwing exaggerated shadows) of the male sculpture looking off to the left, then of the head of a horse looking off to the right, as if pincering him between them in a look.

She comes back in with a heavy cloth sack; he keeps on at her, 'You think this junk's all that matters.' She ignores him. He continues, trying to goad her. 'I've been here before. I've seen them. They're nasty, that's what.' King's little boy is showing: earlier in the arcade, he called Simon 'dirty' for being interested in 'pick-ups'; now, he finds Freya's art — and by implication her sexuality and her identity as a female artist — 'nasty' and lacking in morals. Joan, earlier in this scene, calls herself 'sloppy', a milder adjective that contrasts with King's natty suit; his fastidious approach to his appearance seems all of a piece with his suppressed sexual hang-ups, and Freya's 'sloppiness' and her unvarnished, rough sculptures are a provocation to the young man who lounged so comfortably against the varnished unicorn on the Esplanade.

Figure 6: King and Freya face off

And yet he's fascinated by the sculpture that stands slightly taller than him, a different, anguished representation of the military idea and the violence that he and his gang play with. He can't seem to take his hands off the warrior's chest. As they talk, he moves his hands upwards and puts the index finger and thumb of his left hand into the warrior's eye sockets, probing an absence. Again, with one's Freudian hat on, one might say that he's a little boy playing with a phallus.

'What have my morals got to do with your Joanie?' asks Freya. King, stung, takes his hand away from the head. After a pause he spits at it. Goading her again, but also, in a way, making it 'dirty'.

'Very strange boy,' murmurs Freya and goes out again. Whether it's the accumulation of threatening femaleness that does it, or being confronted explicitly about his childish/virginal state, King is the one now goaded into action. He finds an axe-like tool on a table and goes after Freya.

Outside the birdhouse, the balance of power shifts: King seems freer to act, and the camera freer to move. We cut to a view of the doorway from the outside, and the camera tracks backwards as he comes out. 'I'll show you just how strange I am,' he tells her, eliding the 'boy' epithet that she coupled the adjective with. He raises the little axe. 'Is this what you make your junk with?' he shouts. Cut to Freya, against a background of the outside darkness, visually cut off from her environment.

King backs away, until he sees a sculpture lying prone on the ground (this looks like the same sculpture that Joan touches almost fondly when she and Simon first arrive outside the birdhouse). He swings at it, while she follows after him and protests, 'I don't have anything to do with your Joanie!' Then we cut to the 'head' of the sculpture, which fractures and caves in under King's blows (Losey shows the impact, unlike the similar scene in which Simon was mugged). 'I'll teach you to...' he shouts, and the next phrase is indistinct but seems to include 'your face'.

Freya screams and lunges at him. They roll over to the left, to the very edge of the cliff; the camera pans with them. We cut to a closer shot of King pinning her down. The composition is much more disordered now, a confusion of limbs and clothing. She sobs; he becomes still, and seems to be upset as well. She puts her hand on his arm — an ambiguous gesture. Preparing to push him away? Comforting him?

'You know how much this meaned [sic] to me?' she cries. 'How could you be so cruel?' Then there's a cut to a point of view from beyond the edge of the cliff, beyond the 'brink'. King, his cover blown (and clearly not taking pleasure in the moment, contrary to what most critics have said), gasps: 'I enjoyed it, my dear lady.' His mock-posh idiom is unravelling. He gets to his feet, and the shot cuts on the movement, to a point of view slightly above and to the right, of Freya lying on the cliff. She gets up and shouts: 'I don't believe you!' Wrapping her cardigan around her, in tears, she walks over to her broken sculpture, squats down and picks up one of the fragments.

This latter part of the scene is not in the shooting script; as written, King takes a chisel to a sculpture, declares that he has enjoyed it, then stalks off. The more physical, sexualised confrontation appears to have been improvised on the day. It certainly develops the script's idea — that Freya fears violence to herself far less than violence to her art — into something more visceral and immediate. Lindfors, with her theatrical background and Method-informed acting style, may have had a hand in this; but I also imagine Losey himself, the self-conscious auteur, seeing in the sculpture's mutilation a parallel with the fate of so much of his own work (including, as it turned out, *The Damned*).

Whatever the motivations behind the scene's development, it's all the better for it. Dan Callahan calls this 'the finest scene of Losey's career' (2003), which might be overselling it just a tad (I'd have to plump for the climax of *M* or something from *The Servant*), but it's certainly powerful. It wounds both parties, but its undercurrents are complex: it rejects a straightforward drawing-up of battle lines, for these two are both outsiders, both dealing with the nihilism of their culture, both using violence as a form of expression, yet failing to acknowledge each other as kindred spirits. While King has Freya pinned to the ground, her cardigan falls away to reveal that she's wearing black leather trousers — but the moment of recognition never comes. Has Freya, in effect, called King's bluff, by taking the same material he has been playing with — the aggression, the nihilism, the embrace of wildness, even the black leather — and projecting it back to him as something adult, serious and sexualised? King holds Freya down... then bows his head and crumples, as though he's been found out.

Soon afterwards, in pursuit of Simon and Joan, he begins to climb down the cliff face towards the water. It's as though Freya's sculpture, and Freya herself, have mutated into a vast, sheer and unforgiving surface; he grapples with it, but again it overwhelms him. In a way, King has found in Freya his own Quatermassian monster; Harper and Porter suggest that the *Quatermass* films

> ...inaugurate Hammer's preoccupation, on a symbolic level, with *female* sexuality. In all three films, it is the organism's capacity for exponential reproduction which causes panic in the (male) populace. [...] The monster is a female Proteus, and an index of unconscious fears of the vagina and of the birth process: of the terror evoked by the womb. (2003: 145)

Freya's capacity for reproduction is certainly considerable in terms of her artwork, and she's protean in her methods, reshaping stone and plaster to create hybrid creatures and half-evolved forms. But King's struggles with 'the terror evoked by the womb' are about to reach a new, deeper level.

Footnotes

10. An incident from Frink's childhood makes her involvement with *The Damned* all the more apt: in 1942, while in Exmouth with friends, she was caught up in a German bombing raid.

'We saw all these enemy planes coming in over the sea, and we all fell to the ground. They machine-gunned the parade we were on, and dropped bombs on the road above us. The noise was incredible' (1998: 17). The art shop they had just visited was flattened.
11. In a scene cut from the final film, it's made clear that Bernard still carries a torch for Freya, but that she has moved on.
12. Ironically, Losey himself was susceptible to feeling threatened in this way. His own troubled relationships with women have occasioned comment by those who knew him, including 'Freya' herself, the actress Viveca Lindfors, who told De Rham: 'He was very insecure about women... Joe hated anyone who would not let him be in control' (1991: 123).

Chapter 8: The Living, The Dead And The Damned

The great whatsit

In the popular imagination, atomic weapons were simply too big to deal with; they dominated the horizon, and like the flare from an atomic blast, couldn't be looked at directly. In human-scale dramas they were the killer punchline, as in Robert Aldrich's *Kiss Me Deadly* (1955), when hard-boiled Mike Hammer (Ralph Meeker), having biffed his way through the human detritus of Los Angeles and refusing to hand over the key to a locker that contains a mysterious case, its contents having left him with a strange burn, is left deflated and defeated by Lt Murphy's (Wesley Addy) brief litany: 'Manhattan Project, Los Alamos, Trinity'. Because that's all that needs to be uttered, at this resolution, for the terror to be summoned in the audience. In *The Damned*, nobody even mentions nuclear war or atomic weapons by name, and Bernard speaks in allusions and euphemisms: 'A power has been released that will melt those stones'; 'the destruction that is inevitably coming'; 'after the first great explosion'; and his mantra, 'When the time comes' — a phrase doom-laden enough for Gregory Peck to take it up in *On The Beach* during a discussion about suicide pills.

Euphemism, allusion, understatement... these strategies reduce the subject of apocalypse to a more manageable, more portable and more mysterious thing, a 'great whatsit', as *Kiss Me Deadly*'s Velda (Maxine Cooper) calls it. Radiation answers this requirement: it's invisible, human-scale, insidious, slower in its effects. It shares several qualities with ancient antagonists like bubonic plague, smallpox, or fairy-tale devices like the witch's curse, and it also offers the minimalist chills of announcing its presence not with a bang but with a series of dry clicks on a Geiger counter. More chillingly still, it works its effects on our very core, at the genetic level.

The knowledge that radiation can transform or mutate organic matter predates the coming of the atomic bomb. From Röntgen's discovery of the X-ray in 1895, the phenomenon of radioactivity made a rapid entry into the modern world, with breakthroughs by Becquerel, the Curies and Rutherford following in short order. By 1927, researchers at Columbia University had discovered that subjecting fruit flies to radiation could cause mutations. The practice of radiation breeding began around the same time, firstly on staple crops such as maize and barley; in the 1950s, atomic gardening, partly bolstered by Eisenhower's Atoms for Peace programme, became a mainstream enough activity for a UK Atomic Gardening Society to be established in 1959.[13] Irradiating vegetable seeds with cobalt-60 to produce helpful mutations is one thing; but 1950s popular culture wasn't going to let things rest there.

American B-movies of that decade provide a bestiary packed to bursting with hideously altered creatures. One of the first, *Them!* (1954), featured giant mutated ants in New Mexico after the first atomic bomb test; and scores of others followed suit, usually going unimaginatively for the 'giant mutated' approach as well: *Tarantula* (1955) (a new synthetic food, which has a radioactive isotope as a binding agent, is injected into a spider, among other things); *Monster from Green Hell* (1957) (a rocket full of wasps is exposed to massive amounts of cosmic radiation); *She Demons* (1958) (a Nazi-funded skin treatment involving huge amounts of radiation goes awry); *Attack of the Giant Leeches* (1959) (made thus by radiation from Cape Canaveral)... and so on. Japanese cinema took the genre to another, sometimes visceral level, with *kaiju* films such as *Godzilla/Gojira* (1954) and *Rodan* (1956) replaying the country's atomic calamities in an outlandish key, sometimes, as Kim Newman notes of *Godzilla*, 'going into the nasty details of the catastrophe' (1999: 87). At the bizarre end of Japan's radioactive spectrum were outings like *The H-Man* (1958) and *The Human Vapour* (1960), in which radiation turns humans into avenging blue slime (in the former case) or a cloud of mist (in the latter).

British cinema, with smaller budgets, was unable to compete (with the odd exception such as *Behemoth the Sea Monster* (1959), in which a sea mammal is mutated by radiation into a dinosaur that emits radiation but at least has the decency to be dying slowly from it), although even the most unhinged *kaiju* picture was unequal to the mind of Spike Milligan, whose *The Bed Sitting Room* (1969) has various fallout-infected characters mutating into a parrot, a wardrobe, and the titular single-room dwelling. But by the end of the 1950s, as Kim Newman observes, the 'atomic mutation cycle' of monster movies was losing its hold, especially for the major studios (1999: 91).

Figure 7: Simon and Joan meet the children

But there's an important distinction to made here, and one that feeds directly into *The Damned*: as Susan Sontag, in her classic 1965 study of atomic-age science fiction films, 'The Imagination of Disaster', suggests, much of the appeal of 'creature features' such as *Godzilla* and *Rodan* lie in 'the undeniable pleasure we derive from looking at freaks, at beings excluded from the category of the human' (1965: 45). But there's another kind of science fiction film that *explores* the boundaries between the human and the non-human and questions straightforward distinctions: Victor Carroon in *The Quatermass Xperiment* is a compelling figure because his humanity is at war with the alien nature overcoming him; and in *The Fly* (1958), Dr Delambre (David Hedison) retains his humanity to the extent of engineering his own suicide (as Carroon did in the original TV *Quatermass*) in order to avoid becoming subsumed by the fly's nature. It's this aspect — the disturbing idea of human nature as something that can be mutated and messed with but still self-aware enough not to be disqualified from the category of the human — that moves science fiction closer to horror. The monster in *Frankenstein* is horrific not simply because it is monstrous, but because it is human, and often childlike. In the case of Bernard's children, this is inverted: rather than being monsters undercut by humanity, they are humans tainted by monstrosity.

And who does the tainting? Why, our old friend, the scientist. A number of 1950s films asked us to suppose that a latter-day Frankenstein would seize upon radiation as a new agent in medical procedures boasting variable degrees of vagueness and implausibility: in *The Gamma People* (1955), directed by sometime Hammer employee John Gilling, an Eastern European scientist subjects the youth of his repressive nation-state to gamma rays, turning some of them into prodigies and others into zombies; in *Creature with the Atom Brain* (1955), radiation is somehow used (by a Nazi scientist, naturally) to reanimate the dead in order to provide a gangster with a standing army of mobsters; and in *The Werewolf* (1956), a scientist creates a serum from irradiated wolf blood, believing it will give protection against radioactive fallout, but instead turning his subject into the eponymous beast. This notion of radiation as a virus, like smallpox, that can be used in small amounts to inoculate someone against its own effects, is founded on a fallacy, of course — and it's the same fallacy that underlies the irradiated children in *The Damned*.

One can sense, in this uneasy mix of science and superstition, the struggles of post-war culture to come to terms with the puzzling, sinister new world of nuclear physics. Inevitably, storytellers reach for old symbols and stories, recasting isotopes as viruses, bacteria or other toxins. For example, the children in *The Damned* could be said to resemble ancient archetypes like the Visha Kanya ('poison maidens') of Indian myth who were said to be raised on a diet of poison and antidote in order to become assassins using their own blood and bodily fluids to which they were themselves immune. Nathaniel Hawthorne's use of this legend for his story 'Rappacini's Daughter' (1844) produces something closer in tragic tone to the Losey film: the hero, Giovanni, falls in love with Beatrice, the daughter of a scientist who has grown up among her father's poisonous herb collection and has herself become poisonous, but who, like the children, is otherwise virtuous.[14]

The flaw underground

So how did the children become radioactive and yet immune to their own radioactivity? Bernard's explanation in the film is vague: 'Their mothers were exposed to an unknown kind and level of radiation by an accident' — while pregnant, one assumes. The source novel is a little more forthcoming: the mothers, the book's Bernard explains, were inpatients at a cottage hospital on the south coast when a nearby atomic research station exploded. All the mothers eventually died of radiation sickness, but their babies apparently acquired *in utero*, along with the radioactivity, an immunity to it. It's a feat impossible for living matter, but as we've already established, the living and the non-living are far from clear-cut in *The Damned*.

So there they are, deep inside the cliffs of Portland Bill: the flaw in the script, according to Losey. But this flaw, this paradox of living but deadly tissue, I think expresses something at the heart of cultural attitudes to nuclear and atomic weapons.

Carol Jacobi describes how, for over a year after the dropping of the first atomic bombs on Hiroshima and Nagasaki, heavy censorship ensured that the only imagery from the event to enter widespread circulation was that of the mushroom cloud (2014: 25). And from the very beginning, observer accounts of the cloud betrayed a tendency towards a 'fabulous' idiom that blurred the distinction between living and dead. William L Laurence, who won the 1946 Pulitzer Prize for his eyewitness reporting of the bombing of Nagasaki, described the cloud as 'like a meteor coming from the earth instead of from outer space, becoming ever more alive as it climbed skyward through the white clouds.' Adopting a somewhat triumphalist tone that seems astonishing now, he called it 'a living thing, a new species of being, born right before our incredulous eyes,' and rhapsodised about its 'evolution':

> The mushroom top was even more alive than the pillar, seething and boiling in a white fury of creamy foam, sizzling upwards and then descending earthward, a thousand old faithful geysers rolled into one. (1945)

Laurence's description of the mushroom cloud demonstrates a kind of animism in its ascribing of life to something not just non-living but lethal. Even the phrase 'mushroom cloud' carries a misleading connotation of something living, and Laucht points out that 'mushrooms bore ambivalent meanings and could be associated with either death and decay or magic and life' (2014: 85). Bernard, too, falls for this mythology of living/dead ambivalence when he tells Freya an apocryphal story: 'After the first great explosion, strange wonderful flowers, unknown before, bloomed in the desert'. Freya, the clear-eyed, practising artist having a showdown with the blinkered mandarin, will have none of this grandiose mythmaking; she fires back (or did, until the line was cut): 'You are so in love with death that you are dead yourself'. As they speak, beneath their feet, the living/non-living children have been

Figure 8: King the graveyard bird

reincarcerated after their brief breakout, to continue growing underground like... well, like mushrooms. It's rather a grim twist on the idea of atomic gardening.

The nuclear uncanny

Living/non-living — *The Damned* experiments with this distinction throughout. Freya produces animal and bird sculptures from the local stone, creating a likeness of something living from inert matter; Bernard's children are flesh-and-blood, but the radiation has left their bodies as cold as stone.

Then consider the first time we see King: he lounges against a statue of a unicorn — a fixture on the Esplanade at Weymouth, but a very apposite bit of scenery, a mythical creature, an impossibility, like the stone-cold children. Later, in pursuit of Simon and Joan across the cliffs, King perches in a graveyard, whistling signals to his cronies — like the living embodiment of the 'graveyard bird' sculpture that Freya presents to Bernard in the hotel.

The presence of living birds, in the shape of the local seagulls and some briefly glimpsed swans, is complicated by Freya's bird sculptures, and the introduction of military helicopters at the climax. Losey agreed with Ciment that the sight of the helicopters, 'particularly when we get the three of them, is very sinister' (1985: 202), but he added that Frink's bird sculptures are not straightforward in their meaning: 'they were birds with no wings ... You never feel about those birds that they can take flight'.

The Damned

Flight, as a form of grace, of release, is not easily achieved in *The Damned*; its characters are much more in the habit of falling, whether being mugged, missing a jump to a boat, tumbling over a cliff, or fighting over a defaced sculpture. And the opening sequence announces as much when the pan comes to rest on one of Frink's 'Falling Man' sculptures — non-living commentary on the living who are about to fall.

The living/non-living distinction becomes more complicated still when Simon and Joan are rescued by the children and taken into the caves. For a start, this act of rescue paradoxically condemns the pair to death, as any proximity to the radioactive children does; and when Joan takes the hand of one of the girls, it's the latter's hand that feels icy cold rather than Joan's, despite her having just been pulled from the sea. Thus, the film chalks up another incongruity: radioactivity, usually associated with heat (it burns down a beach house in *Kiss Me Deadly*, for heaven's sake), has made the children's bodies cold. Victoria cries in wonder at Joan's warmth; but in this strange underground pocket of nuclear absurdity, warmth means not life but, in the presence of the children, a death sentence.

King's arrival brings more irony: after their last meeting, his muttered promise to the departing Simon was 'Next time I see you ... you're a dead man,' a B-movie cliché, but prophetic. Now, after touching the chilly face of one of the boys, he gasps in horror: 'He's dead, I tell you!' But it's truer of himself than of the boy, since King is now, like Simon and Joan, beginning to be affected by the children's radiation. The latter, meanwhile, are busily projecting their own lethal attributes onto their captors, referring to the radiation-suited military as 'the Black Death'.

Death, or a death-in-life, permeates this militarised landscape. At the same time, above ground, a member of King's gang has been caught and asks his captors: 'What kind of establishment is this, then? A morgue?' A mere minute earlier, Simon and Joan have fled through a graveyard and entered the military compound, whose obelisk-like concrete blocks resemble smooth modernist gravestones — and now we're in familiar Hammer territory: the Gothic mode, complete with a night-time cemetery, a misguided scientist, a secret laboratory and a nest of lethal, man-made monsters.

As must be obvious by now, the presence of a graveyard is much more than an atmospheric conceit, or even a box-ticking exercise to suture it into the body of Hammer Films. It's easily read as a reference to the 'buried' children whose death-in-life status is causing such an upset at the centre of the film, but in the context of historical narratives of the time concerning the Cold War and nuclear weapons, its evocation of Hammer's familiar Gothic territory completes the link from the nineteenth-century notion of the uncanny to a twentieth-century one.

'The nuclear age,' writes anthropologist Joseph Masco, 'has witnessed the apotheosis of the uncanny' (2006: 27). Masco coined the phrase 'the nuclear uncanny' to describe the sense of 'dislocation and anxiety' that characterises the Cold War psyche. These words reach back to Freud's famous essay 'The Uncanny', in which he states:

> To many people the acme of the uncanny is represented by anything to do with death, dead bodies, revenants, spirits and ghosts [...] in some modern languages the German phrase 'ein unheimliches Haus' [...] can be rendered only by the periphrasis 'a haunted house.' (1919: 148)

Masco describes Freud's conception of the uncanny as 'that which blurs the distinction between the living and the dead, the hallucinatory and the real, and which, in essence, makes sensory experience untrustworthy and strange' (2006: 28). He goes on to point out:

> Radiation is colorless and odorless, yet capable of affecting living beings at the genetic level. In this sense, nuclear materials produce the uncanny effect of blurring the distinction between the animate and the inanimate, and between the natural and the supernatural. (2006: 30)

Another of the key components of the uncanny that Freud identified is the 'return of the repressed' via the reappearance of 'something that was long familiar to the psyche and was estranged from it only through being repressed' (1919: 148). And there are several forms of repression that have significance, I think, for the compelling strangeness of the children. First is Freud's own reference to 'the idea of being buried alive', of which he says 'this terrifying fantasy is merely a variant of another, which was originally not at all frightening [...] the fantasy of living in the womb' (1919: 150). Second is the supposed banishment of superstition and irrational beliefs in the 'age of science', only to emerge again in some of the grotesque conceptions of nuclear physics that I've already mentioned (Laurence's 'living' mushroom cloud, for example, and the swathe of bizarre mutated-monster flicks). And third is the historical moment, which I mentioned in Chapter 4, when the Limited Test Ban Treaty forced nuclear testing underground, effectively *repressing* both the activity and any evidence of it. I imagine the nine 'buried alive' children as the uncanny offspring of these forms of repression, now returned to wreak havoc on logic, nature and the texture of Losey's film.

Bernard's plan, though, is to end this repression, but only when all else is destroyed. He explains to Freya: 'When that time comes, the thing itself will open up the door and my children will go out to inherit the Earth.' Hammer had actually visited this idea before, courtesy of Nigel Kneale, who adapted his own television play, *The Creature* (1955), into *The Abominable Snowman* (1957). Towards the end of the film, Dr Rollason (Peter Cushing) is having a rethink about the shaggy creatures he and Dr Friend (Forrest Tucker) have encountered in the Himalayas:

> ROLLASON: Suppose they're not just a pitiable remnant waiting to die out. They're waiting, yes, but waiting for us to go.
>
> FRIEND: For mankind to die out?
>
> ROLLASON: There was something the Llama said about taking thought for man's successors...

Another set of ice-cold creatures awaiting mankind's destruction, then. When Friend demands what sort of survival the creatures can hope for in the ice-bound wastes, Rollason, echoing Bernard's refrain, replies: 'It's enough, until perhaps their time comes.'

The complicated games that *The Damned* plays with ideas of living, dead and non-living, and the central contradiction of radioactive living beings, are not, as Losey thought, the unforgivable flaw in *The Damned*; they are the indispensable core of a film that, more boldly than most cinema of the era, deals in the nuclear uncanny and its human consequences. It dramatises the absurdity of Cold War logic as practiced by the nuclear state — an absurdity expressed many times, but summed up thus by Masco: '...in order to prevent an apocalypse the governmental apparatus has prepared [...] meticulously to achieve it' (2006: 12). The children, with their life that is no life, represent the political state of existence that Orwell, in 'You and the Atomic Bomb', described as a 'peace that is no peace' (1945: 10).

Footnotes

13. Historical context for early work on radiation is supported by material in Hogg (2016) (see 'Bibliography). Background on radiation breeding and atomic gardening is supported by the Genome News Network (www.genomenewsnetwork.org/resources/timeline/1927_Muller.php).
14. I am indebted to Pam Lock for introducing me to the 'poison maidens' tradition in literature. Details and context were sourced from Wikipedia (en.wikipedia.org/wiki/Visha_Kanya). See also Oliver Wendel Holmes' novel *Elsie Venner* (1861), which does something similar with snake venom.

Chapter 9: The Heart of Darkness

The bunker beneath the Edgecliff Establishment has properties reminiscent of other cinematic spaces that exert a strange influence beyond their boundaries: the ocean planet in Tarkovsky's *Solaris* (1972), the Zone in his *Stalker* (1979), Kurtz's compound in Coppola's *Apocalypse Now* (1979). They're a modern rendition of the fairy-tale realm of enchantment or Lewis Carroll's Looking-Glass world, where logic and causality lose their influence and even the laws of physics can be compromised. *The Damned* is a journey into the heart of darkness, all the darker for its location a stone's throw from the gaudy lights of a seaside resort.

That strange influence, as I suggested, is at work from the very outset. It's as though all the intense behaviour we've witnessed is being caused by it. Simon and Joan are pulled together inexorably despite their apparent incompatibility; Bernard rents his outhouse to his ex-lover despite the huge security risk; King and Freya circle each other, collide, and fly apart.

Initially, the children's location is a puzzle: Bernard's first address to them leaves the spatial relations in doubt, and it takes us a while to get our bearings. It's only when Simon and Joan tumble over the cliff that things start to fall into place. Even then, the warren of caves and passages feels somehow unmappable, despite the brief appearance in one scene of a scale model. It's an apt disorientation, perhaps, since the deeper we go into the mystery of the children the harder it is to figure out where we are. Contributing to this feeling of discontinuity is the fact that, of course, none of these spaces are really *there*: the main complex was constructed in a studio, and the caves and passageways were either found at different points along the local coastline or built up from fibreglass and polystyrene. A retrospective article about the filming in the *Dorset Echo* preserves this sense of displacement nicely: various witnesses recall seeing 'caves ... built on the footpath ... and dug out by the film company' and 'fibreglass rocks made to look like Portland stone' (2008). Naturally, this is all standard filmmaking practice, but the punchline is that, as I mentioned in Chapter 4, there *was* a nuclear bunker in roughly the place that the fictional bunker is supposed to be.

The shooting script explains that the children's hideout is 'a cave left over from an old pumping installation'. A door at sea level provides the route for Simon and Joan's entry; what we don't yet see, adding to the disorientation of this space, is how the children can leave the caves to retrieve them from the water. The first exchanges between the children and the adults, and the oddly furnished little grotto they are taken to, are all the more unworldly because of the missing transition: it's a continuation of the mode of experience that the couple have been in since climbing through Freya's window (when Simon called the birdhouse 'a fabulous place'). It takes King's arrival for the more prosaic matter of whys and hows to be explained.

Foremost of the hows is the door, which is activated from outside by radiation. This is to be the mechanism of release for the children, triggered by the fallout from the 'inevitable' apocalypse. It's one of the plot's more glaring holes — literally — that they can already escape via the grated window, and that, unless the great conflagration also does away with the sea, they'll still be as trapped as before. That the film doesn't collapse in on itself with this inconsistency is reminiscent of the dilemma of the trapped-but-not-really guests in Luis Buñuel's *The Exterminating Angel* (1962), and another measure of just how absurd the climate inside the Project has become.

A further sign of the Through-the-Looking-Glass nature of the bunker is the opening that the children refer to as 'the screen' — not the video screen, but a window onto the sea that they take turns looking through. A glimpse of the 'real' is a carefully rationed treat for these sequestered creatures; meanwhile Bernard keeps watch over them via his own screen several times a day.

The complex's main area is space-age but drab, austere and functional: a long, sectioned chamber with smooth surfaces and modernist furniture. Geometry rules this place: rectangles predominate, in the grid of tape machines on the walls, the rows of desks in the classroom, the metal shelves, the partitions between areas, and the blackboards, bearing scrawled logarithms, that flank the most prominent rectangle of all — the video screen, Bernard's pulpit. Even the art is confined here: along the far wall, hung at regular intervals, are reproductions of old paintings, each framed and mounted on a rectangular column. No dangerously unconfined sculpture here; when Freya's graveyard bird looms behind Bernard's head, it, too, is safely contained by the frame of the video screen. The children's science lab, contrastingly, bristles with objects far more obviously dangerous but out in the open: glass tubing, retorts, Bunsen burners, bottles of chemicals.

We see the classroom area a handful of times before Losey gives us a walk-through of the whole place, in a sequence lasting almost two minutes from the trip down in the lift to the arrival in the dormitory area at the far end. To my knowledge, no other Hammer film has an extended sequence like this — although the shadows and the atmospherics turn the complex into something like the 'old dark house' of the Gothic horror genre.

Freya's birdhouse was disclosed to us in stages, through the characters' interactions inside it; the bunker is laid out, in this sequence, clinically and without interruption (what looks like a single shot is actually composed of at least two, possibly three, shots spliced together on the dark partitions between the areas). Where the sound in the birdhouse was the quiet rustle of the sea, here it's the low hum of machinery and the slow footsteps of the radiation-suited Major Hammond, our POV for the walk-through (on 'his nightly patrol', the shooting script explains). We see the bunker through Hammond's eyes, but we also experience his approach from the point of view of the children: he spins a large school globe with his gloved hand as he passes, suggesting the control that these adults have on their 'world' (and making a visual rhyme with King's gloved hand on the wall before Simon's mugging). A rising drumbeat plays in time with his footsteps, like a stalking monster from a Hammer creature feature, reaching a crescendo by the time Hammond reaches the dormitory area; Henry cowers in his bed as Hammond, the Black Death, looks down on him. And well might the children give these sinister beings such a name: two of their number, we are told, have died from the effects of their own radiation, and were, one assumes, carried away by a hazmat-clad figure. Now Mary, too, is showing similar symptoms.

Fable, fantasy, the irrational, the irregular: these things cannot be denied, and can only be contained for so long. Bernard, whose appreciation of art and love affair with Freya have already signalled a certain conflict in his nature, allows the children their surveillance-free 'hideout', against the objections of Hammond and others ('The mental health of the children is more important than your ideas of security'). This is Bernard's weakness, a sentimental leaning that he presents as a necessity for the children's psychological wellbeing. The hideout has to exist for the plot mechanics to operate, but it's as much a flaw in the script as the children's radioactivity. And it's this secret, irregular space — the cave near the water's edge where Simon and Joan are first taken — that allows for the non-oblong, the ungoverned and the fanciful. Like Freya's birdhouse, its rough-hewn surroundings provide a setting for expression and creation: here the children have 'invented' their parents using old magazine pictures, and tell stories about their situation. 'We're on a huge spaceship and we're going to a star,' William hypothesises, indulging in the sort of science fiction that *The Damned* definitely isn't. Of the invented parents, the shooting script observes: 'In each case the couple cannot possibly be man and wife because they are from different periods of history'. When Simon asks Victoria about their parents, she replies: 'We were hoping *you* were our parents', as though this latest unlikely couple, from different generations if not different historical periods, seems to fit their invented universe. And notice how Simon and Joan, ensconced in the hideout with their towels and dressing gowns, are visually recreating the aftermath of their tryst in Freya's bed, as though they, too, are following some urge to create, or recreate, a couple-unit.

The hideout may be empowering for the children, but it has the opposite effect on the adults they bring to it. No sooner has King entered via the sea door than he mutters 'Forward into battle, dear chaps', but this time without conviction; something about this environment begins to drain King of his bluster. It's killing him, in a literal sense, but it's also doing something metaphorical to him — something that began with his exposure to Freya's birdhouse. First he has grappled with the cliff ('like a fly on a wall', says the shooting script), then he falls into the sea, and again is overwhelmed, swallowed up. Now he is rescued by Henry, a mere child, who takes him into the tunnel, where his overpowering continues. He confronts Simon, but the little he manages to summon in terms of rage is quickly stifled — by his own unease, by the onset of radiation sickness, and by the whole environment in which he's now imprisoned. Earlier, Joan had described how her brother locked her in a cupboard for showing interest in a man; now King is trapped in a cave with Joan *and* a man she's done a good deal more than show interest in. He's an orphan surrounded by orphans

The Damned

(who can open a door that he can't), a sexually insecure man enclosed in a womb-like space, a gang leader separated from his gang and losing ground to an older man who has taken up with his sister. If it's possible to be disempowered to death, King is well on the way.

Paul Mayersberg remarked of the final-reel fate of the doomed child-molester in Losey's remake of *M*: 'He is now underground and can fall no further' (1963: 34). For King, the descent isn't quite over.

Figure 9: Simon, Joan and a fallen King

Chapter 10: Violent Reactions and Absurd Heroics

The 'climactic' scenes of escape lose some impact through what looks like a lessening of interest on Losey's part: the camera hangs back, the angles and compositions are less considered. This part of the shooting script bears the heaviest burden of pencilled notes, mostly concerning the logistical demands of plot (never Losey's strong point): who should stand where, and what should happen to the guard's machine gun? Bernard's last screen address to the children, though, is nicely done, with Freya's graveyard bird casting a shadow behind him. Losey even manages to fit in a Martin Luther reference when one of the boys throws an inkwell at Bernard's face on the screen (presumably an allusion to the story in which Luther throws one at the Devil in his cell).

In amongst the necessary exposition and the rescue-related fussing, King's world continues to collapse. Having had his manly play-acting exposed by Freya as naive and clueless, he is now faced with the military reality that his mock-army imitated for sport: forced to shoot a guard dead, he reacts with horror. Simon has already established his supremacy over King by keeping a cool head in the caves; now King has been not only dethroned but demoted to the rank of footsoldier.

Not that Simon is reigning supreme. Forced by circumstances out of the role of uncommitted liberal, he soon discovers that the certainties of the last war, in which, we have to assume, he saw active service, are no longer any basis for action. Bernard greeted him with a lament about the senselessness of modern violence; now he is confronted with something worse: not senseless, but in thrall to the absurd calculations of Cold War logic.

Simon himself, when he finally realises that the children are radioactive, is made to understand the folly of liberating them: 'You can't do that,' snaps Hammond, 'they're dangerous!' Simon pauses, removes his hand from a boy's shoulder, but then a girl runs forward and throws her arms around him, crying 'Please, Simon, take us out! Please take us out!' That, and Hammond's insistent 'You can't do this — you can't!' stiffen Simon's resolve. 'Can't I?' he mutters, seemingly goaded by Hammond into pressing on with his heroism regardless. It's an absurd move, if he really understands the repercussions, but we've already established that this is an absurd dimension; and it mirrors his fateful decision on the Esplanade: the children, like Joan, have lured him into a rash act that will end badly. For Simon, Joan and King, there's no way out of this impasse, and the film's title acquires another layer of connotation: damned if you do, damned if you don't.

Figure 10: No way out: reality dawns on Simon, Joan and King

The problematic nature of Simon's heroism validates Colin Gardner's assessment of *The Damned* as 'perhaps Losey's most direct expression of action-realism's bankruptcy' (2004: 109); Losey himself, speaking to Tom Milne, traced the development of his attitude to the heroic stance and its ability to effect change:

> When I began to make films in Hollywood, I had not only full confidence, but an absolute delight in stating issues I saw to be true, with perfect faith that they were soluble and that I could contribute to their solution. The world isn't so simple. (1968: 41)

It seems appropriate that *The Damned*, with its insistent refusal of easy 'action-realism' solutions, should appear in Losey's resumé just when his career was about to transition from plot-driven genre pictures to character-driven arthouse works. But that doesn't help us as viewers during the latter half of *The Damned*. The children are released, only to be rounded up and re-incarcerated — genies returned to the bottle, Pandora's Box restocked and slammed shut again. This is not what we expect of a rescue plot. But what else could happen? The children are innocent, so they can't be destroyed like the staring, pudding-bowl-haircut aliens in *The Village of The Damned*; but they're deadly, so what would their escape mean? How can we make sense of the heroic failure to rescue the children?

I can offer several suggestions that, at least partially, fit with the larger narrative and with the terms of Losey's film-making at this point. Firstly, for the children it enacts a kind of fall, just as the other characters have fallen, but in this case it's a fall from innocence or ignorance. Bernard, realising this, laments '...my children will now see themselves as prisoners and as freaks'. Secondly, it leaves us in no doubt as to the ruthlessness and effectiveness of the state-sanctioned violence. And thirdly, in a film that has been drawing circles since the very first shot, here at the centre is the tightest, and the cruellest, circular motion of all.

Simon and Joan never hear Bernard's explanation about the reasons for cultivating the radioactive children so carefully; they are shepherded back to the boat without further comment. This, whether down to clumsiness in the plotting or something more intentional, is a radical departure from the norm, according to which the investigating hero, as a stand-in for the audience, uncovers the truth about the machinations of the villain. 'The people who know all the answers are much happier,' he told Freya at their first meeting; but, he added, 'I don't like the answers'. Is this why he doesn't press Bernard to explain — an existential objection to finding out? Jones and Losey evidently struggled with the question of how Simon and Joan should handle their dawning realisation that they have stumbled into something bigger than they can handle; the shooting script includes a decidedly unheroic speech by Simon:

> I don't know what it is you're doing, except that it is vicious and evil. I don't want to know. I don't want any part of it. I just want to be away from whatever you're doing. Do you want me to beg you? ... I have a boat ... I'll go to France ... I'll go anywhere ... let us go!

It's not surprising that this was cut, but the general sense of his resignation remains (although Jones and Losey aren't finished with them yet). It's in line with the tendency that Paul Mayersberg identifies:

> The desire for peace in escape has been a deep and consistent theme in Losey's work [...] The inner conflict that tortures many of Losey's heroes is between fighting to attain peace and merely giving in when the fight proves too difficult. (1963: 32)

Earlier, lying with Joan on Freya's bed, Simon told her: 'I've never found this kind of quietness before. It's as if I were no longer afraid of dying.' It's Mayersberg's 'peace in escape', but it's also illusory; there is no peace in escape, as the couple discover at the very end. And we circle back to Orwell's phrase as he tried to articulate the paradoxes of the Cold War: a 'peace that is no peace'.

The only character to retain a principled stand in the face of Bernard's revelations is Freya. Perhaps this is why, in her final scene, she dons a white hat — a floppy sunhat, like Simon's in the opening scene. Not only that, but she also helps to trace another circular movement: when Bernard shoots her, she embodies, or even becomes, the 'falling man' sculpture of hers that we saw at the beginning, and, here at the end, becomes a falling woman.

And how much more effective it would have been, had Freya been cut down by a helicopter, as Losey intended — had the themes of flight, terror and surveillance found their final expression in an act of mechanised, airborne, impersonal violence. So how can we make sense of Bernard being her executioner? He is symbolically snuffing out the last signs of his humanity by murdering his ex-lover, of course. But there's another possible interpretation: yes, perhaps Bernard is silencing her, but he was happy enough to let Simon and Joan leave. They are dying from radiation poisoning, but Freya will soon be, too — one of the children ran straight into her arms, and Freya held her for a few moments. The implication, after Hammond's own exposure, is that fleeting contact is all it takes. So, is Bernard carrying out a mercy killing? That's a stretch. His killing of Freya at that moment makes him finally irredeemable; he has just, in her words, wasted whatever time she had left.[15]

King, meanwhile, is completing his trajectory, driving away in Freya's car (with Henry an insistent passenger) and getting weaker by the moment. The cause on a narrative level is radiation sickness, but a contributing factor may be his occupying this female space — a woman's sports car instead of his manly motorcycle — with a child clinging on to him. The helicopters in pursuit are like Freya's bird sculptures come to life as avenging furies; Henry, who has attached himself to King as a father figure, creates another kind of torment for him. Beset all at once by an airborne enemy, radiation sickness and an emotionally needy child, and still reeling from the paradoxical universe inside the bunker, King begins to unravel into contradictory outbursts. 'Look after yourself', he tells Henry, then 'You're poison! You're killing me!' Finally, with Henry grabbed back by the Black Death, King crashes Freya's car through the barrier, and this time the water, which seems to have been lying in wait for him since the very first frame of the film, swallows him up.[16]

Figure 11: King's death plunge

The final turn

But we're not done yet. Most accounts of the ending suggest that Simon's boat drifts out to sea with its doomed occupants, while helicopters circle overhead. But that isn't what happens: the heroic has one last hurrah.

At first their conversation is resigned, defeated, escapist. 'We can go back to the beginning,' says Simon (another circular reference). The shooting script gives him a longer speech about how he wants to take Joan to the warm south and show her 'the terraced vineyards [...] and white houses in the sun'. He goes on: 'We'll find an island off the Grecian coast, where there's only a little village, with an old temple on the hill, and goats climbing through the ruins.'

Joan replies (as she does in the finished film): 'We can't leave the children.' The direction reads: 'Simon looks at her, and knows that she is right, goes to the wheel and puts the boat about.' Onscreen, it's clear from the wake of the keel, and from how the aerial shot pans ahead of them to the clifftop, that this is their new heading.

Any second attempt at rescue will end in a second failure, but Simon and Joan are about to attempt it anyway. Why? Because the alternative — leaving the children — is unthinkable. Action-realism may be bankrupt, but the moral instinct, the sense of right and wrong, still functions. And, like Freya ('You are wasting whatever time I have left'), they react to news of their imminent demise with a final act of defiance, by beginning something that they can't possibly end.

Is this what the 'more full of hope' note in the shooting script means (see Chapter 3)? Andrew Sarris identified in Losey's work 'that psychic spasm, that futile gesture a character makes to register a personal protest against cosmic injustice' (1968: 97). The hope, perhaps, lies in this instinct, in which Losey believed — the reflex towards the good, the heroic. It's still a bit of a stretch, and there's no denying the downbeat tone of the ending. But there's another sort of spasm, an instinct that Losey hasn't quite finished obeying: the circular movement. Simon turns the boat around, heading back to shore; the helicopter follows (more circles busily keeping it in the air). After Freya's murder, there's a pan from the rocks outside the cave door out to sea, reversing the direction of the pan in the film's title sequence. The penultimate shot takes us back to the beginning, with a view of Weymouth Esplanade from out at sea, this time not to the clangour of a rock 'n' roll pastiche but to the cries of the children, pleading to be rescued. Bleak indeed; but shapely. Losey liked topping and tailing things with a circular pattern so much that he used it again in his next film, *Eve*, and again in *Accident*. The final shot, over the closing credits, reprises the doomed, absurd heroism of Simon and Joan's bid to return to the children: the boat, the watching helicopter ('a great mechanical vulture' says the shooting script), and on the soundtrack, no music, only the sound of the helicopter's blades, until that, too, fades out.

Figure 12: Simon and Joan head back to shore, pursued by helicopter

The bleakness, which still seemed fairly strong, dark stuff in 1963, only took a couple more years to percolate into mainstream cinema in films such as *The Spy Who Came In From The Cold* (1965) and *Seconds* (1966), which end with the unglamorous deaths of their protagonists. A few years further on, and the post-sixties paranoia of political thrillers like *Klute* (1971), *The Parallax View* (1974) and *The Conversation* (1974) would take up the refrain of *The Damned* and show the powers that be surveilling the hell out of their citizens and asserting themselves with high-tech ruthlessness in the name of protecting the Free World.

Footnotes

15. There's one other possible motivation: among the lines for this scene in the shooting script that were later cut, there's a plea from Bernard to Freya: 'If you will only understand me, we can rebuild what we had together'. Like Simon with Joan, he wants to circle back to the beginning. Does her final rejection of him lead to a 'crime of passion'? Again, a stretch.
16. An extra shot in the script would have tied up a loose end: 'SID on his motorcycle stops by the broken railing. He looks in the direction of the helicopter and then roars away toward Weymouth. The helicopter banks as, vulture-like, it begins to follow SID.'

Chapter II: After-Effects

The component parts of *The Damned* flew apart, and like the nuclei of unstable atoms, they decayed at differing rates. The film itself has decayed the least; its 2010 DVD release shows the print to be in fine shape, even if — as Marcus Hearn explains in the viewing notes — it's now something of a hybrid itself, with footage restored to approximate the UK version but the opening credits proclaiming the US title *These Are The Damned* (Hearn explains that 'the original British titles for the film are sadly not preserved' (2010: 23)).

Unlike many cult films, *The Damned* hasn't become a staple of late-night screenings or the subject of internet memes. It hasn't had its canonising moment as a cultural reference on *The Simpsons* or *South Park*. But it does strike a spark or two of recognition, when it's not being confused with *Village of the Damned* or *Children of the Damned*. A friend responded to my humming a few bars of 'Black Leather Rock' with 'Hang on — my mate was always singing that but he had no idea where it was from! I'm going to text him.' Slim pickings, posterity-wise. On hearing the title, a few film-conversant friends could reach back murmuringly and emerge with 'Radioactive kids underground...? Bikers?' To be fair, a few were prompt with variations on 'Oh, sure — strange thing that completely changes in the middle. He did it just before *The Servant*.' And my favourite remark: 'Don't they stuff the kids back into the cliff at the end?' But there's no arguing with the upturn in its reputation; many surveys of cinema now align with the judgement of Glenn Erickson at Turner Classic Movies that '[w]hat was once considered one of Joseph Losey's weakest efforts is quickly becoming recognized as the very best of English Science Fiction filmmaking'.[17]

The late Philip French could claim some early credit for spotting its qualities. In one of his last *Guardian* pieces he recounted receiving a letter from Losey after his positive review of *The Damned*: '"Thank you," he said, "for praising it and not for overpraising it.... This has changed the situation for myself and my associates."' French was puzzled until he heard that Losey had just made a film called *The Servant* 'on a small budget with everybody deferring their payments [...] And what he was saying was that my review had prepared people for it — he'd never made a film in Britain that had much appealed to British critics' (2013).

Joseph Losey reached the exalted world he seemed to be hankering after, the art-movie sphere of the likes of Antonioni and Resnais. But by 1970, he was, the consensus would have it, played out, his health deteriorating after years of heavy drinking and mental strain. Imagery from *The Damned* sometimes resurfaced in his later work (obsessive revisiting of imagery is often cited as a trait of the auteur, although all directors probably indulge in it to some extent): there's something of Portland Bill in the villain Gabriel's island hideout in *Modesty Blaise*, and in Sissy Goforth's retreat in *Boom!* (which also begins with a rugged-coastline credits sequence, except that this time, the camera is looking out from *inside* an edifice, as though Losey himself is taking shelter inside a bunker of some kind). *Modesty Blaise* also features modern art in abundance, including an armless sentinel-figure overlooking the sea that half-recalls one of Frink's sculptures in *The Damned*; and Mrs Fothergill (Rosella Falk) has a distinct kinship with Freya Neilson, albeit in a crueller, more misogynist key (Viveca Lindfors was approached to play her but declined, according to Edith De Rham (1991: 169)). Losey's First World War drama *King and Country* (1964) begins with a sequence that restates *The Damned*'s ironic opening commentary on the British establishment: a pan across the details of the war memorial at Hyde Park Corner (made from Portland stone), followed by a dissolve to the muck and chaos of the trenches. Losey never went near science fiction again, and despite claiming, in his interview with Ciment, to have been approached by Michael Carreras several times to work for Hammer again, he never did (1985: 199).

'[H]e didn't live up to his promise,' was Viveca Lindfors' verdict to De Rham (1991: 123). Alexander Knox agreed; he told the same writer: 'He could have been a Billy Wilder, a Visconti or whatever, but something held him back. He was always on the brink of commercial success, pulling back at the last minute' (1991: 123-124).

There's that phrase again: the brink.

As for Lindfors herself, she continued her career on stage and occasionally screen, but in 1990 she suffered an incident that recalled the beginning of *The Damned* when she was attacked by a gang in New York. She said of the incident, echoing Bernard's words: '...It was pure violence, pure violence, and that's disturbing.' One of her final roles was in another science fiction film, *Stargate* (1994).[18]

Oliver Reed, as hardly anyone over the age of 30 needs telling, became a major star in the later sixties, and increasingly a self-parody thereafter. He was often cast in similar 'troubled thug/gang leader' roles, and often in island or coastal locations, for example in *Paranoiac* and *The Shuttered Room* (1967). Shirley Anne Field overcame the criticism that dogged the beginning of her career and, after working for most of the 1970s on the stage, had a film resurgence with *My Beautiful Launderette* (1985). Her memoir, *A Time for Love*, makes for an interesting companion piece to Lindfors' *Viveca... Viveka*; both show their authors as inquisitive, open-hearted 'seekers', although Field's might set some kind of record for name-dropping.

Knox, besides continuing his acting career, became a successful novelist. One late role saw him returning to the murky world of establishment secrecy: in the BBC's John le Carré adaptation *Tinker, Tailor, Soldier, Spy* (1979), Knox played the head of the Circus, the MI6-like intelligence agency, a character known only — and after Knox's repressive patriarch in *The Damned*, quite resonantly — as Control.

Hammer's science fiction output dwindled after *The Damned*, as its gothic horror productions took over (largely at the behest of American co-producers who had only to gesture towards the box-office returns for the *Frankenstein* and *Dracula* sequels). A final Quatermass film, *Quatermass and the Pit* (1967), featured an occult element that nudged it closer to Hammer's main stable. *Moon Zero Two* (1969), Hammer's bid to cash in on the upcoming Apollo mission to the moon (and promoted as 'the first space western'), fared badly at the box office; it couldn't help but look rather small-time in the wake of Kubrick's game-changing *2001: A Space Odyssey* (1968).[19]

In 1963, the year *The Damned* was finally released in the UK, Elisabeth Frink finished a bronze sculpture inspired, she said, by watching Laurence Olivier in *Richard III*. It followed the theme of the falling man that she had pursued for some years. She titled it *Dying King*.[20]

In the 1970s, the BBC produced a number of dramas, such as *Survivors* (1975–77) and *The Changes* (1975), that used science fiction to address some of the same socio-political concerns about crisis and authority. A decade later, the secret workings of the state in nuclear matters were the subject of sustained fictional treatment in dramas such as *Threads* (1984) and *Edge of Darkness* (1985) — and Peter Watkins'

1965 film *The War Game* was finally aired. The idea of humanity emerging from underground after a nuclear war to evolve into a new, superior race of radiation-resistant beings found its way into young adult fiction such as Louise Lawrence's *Children of the Dust* (1985). More recently, the subculture of conspiracy theories concerning experimentation on humans, especially children (for a taste, just google 'Montauk Project' — or, more sensibly, don't), has filtered into the mainstream, for example in TV dramas such as *The X Files* (1993-2002; 2016-18), *Fringe* (2008-13) and *Stranger Things* (2016-).

Government establishments of the 1950s and 1960s, with their now-crumbling brutalist architecture and air of sinister secrecy, have in a way become for modern sensibilities what ruined and mouldering churches were for the nineteenth-century Romantics (and, by extension, the producers at Hammer): a subject for reflections and intimations of mortality and dread, but also symbols of the beauty of decay and obsolescence. Orford Ness in Suffolk, one of the most significant such establishments, is now a National Trust property, and an icon of the newish (cult)ural trends of hauntology or psychogeography. Had WG Sebald lived to consider the resonances of the Jurassic Coast, he may well have had some thoughts about that peculiar prominence on the tail end of Chesil Beach.

Much in the same way that, in centuries past, a traveller might stop at a country inn and hear tales of local hauntings, eerie farmhouses and sunken villages, the twenty-first-century wayfarer can come across a bloke in a pub whose cousin has a mate who owns some land that includes the blocked-up entrance to an old nuclear bunker or ROTOR radar station. Sometimes, as at Kelvedon Hatch, secret nuclear culture is co-opted by the counterculture to stage music events in decommissioned facilities; in the case of the Portland ROTOR bunker, groups such as Subterranea Britannica (as well as more 'freelance' explorers) have investigated what remains of the facility, and the photographs confirm that the reality falls far short of Richard MacDonald's designs for the bunker in *The Damned*. Access is now permanently blocked, however, for safety reasons: not radioactivity, but that other twentieth-century peril — asbestos.[21]

Footnotes

17. http://www.tcm.com/this-month/article.html?isPreview=&id=939244%7C160860&name=These-Are-the-Damned
18. These details are sourced from a news article in the *LA Times*, in which she also remarked, Freya-like: 'This kid must have been very passionate, very turbulent, and if you could channel that quality into something creative, he might become a very important human being'. (http://articles.latimes.com/1990-01-14/news/mn-283_1_actress-viveca-lindfors). Accessed 1-05-2017.
19. This kind of historical and filmographic information for Hammer Films is supported by the great triumvirate of Hammer history: Hearn and Barnes (2007), Meikle (1996) and Kinsey (2002). See 'Bibliography'.
20. http://www.tate.org.uk/art/artworks/frink-dying-king-t07395
21. Some helpful information about the Portland bunker in its current state is online at Subterranea Britannica (www.subbrit.org.uk/rsg/sites/p/portland). Accessed 1-5-2017.

Appendix: Stray Elements

Nothing about *The Damned* is neat; one of its lessons is that there's no such thing as a closed system. There are always leaks, spillages, escapes. Writing about the film, I've found, creates a similar effect: items of significance are left without a comfortable place in the narrative. So here they are: stray elements left over after the experiment.

Umbrellas, hats, sun cream, insurance

We've already acknowledged the absurdity of relying on atomic and nuclear weapons for national protection; the principal characters in *The Damned* all rely on protection of one kind or another. Call it an intentional conceit, or call it a series of minor coincidences.

Both King and Bernard carry an umbrella: a symbol of the establishment and conformity, but also an indication of preparedness — something to be deployed 'when the time comes'. Its associations are many: the British Prime Minister Neville Chamberlain, who often carried one, was sometimes depicted in political cartoons as an umbrella (suggesting, perhaps, an inadequate preparation for a violent storm); and the British journalist Wilfred Burchett, whose 1945 *Daily Express* article, 'The Atomic Plague', broke news of the radiation effects of the atomic bomb, was famous for having taken an umbrella on his journey to Hiroshima. Carol Jacobi suggests that two 1946 paintings by Francis Bacon, *Painting* (1946) and *Study for Man with Microphones* (subsequently reworked as *Gorilla with Microphones* and later partially destroyed), both of which feature black umbrellas, may allude both to Chamberlain and to Burchett (2014: 36).

Both Simon and Freya are seen wearing white sun hats; perhaps signifying their good-guy status, but also protecting them against radiation — from the sun, but radiation nonetheless. Likewise, Joan, once aboard Simon's boat, begins applying sun cream, another measure of protection that will prove futile against the radiation she is about to encounter.

King, in his first few scenes, is equipped with gloves; Losey draws attention to them just before the mugging by having King lay a gloved hand against a wall as he lies in wait. This expresses something about King's insulated existence, something that he will lose soon enough (along with the gloves, which aptly disappear from his hands on the way to his encounter with Freya). Three key moments during his later downfall involve King touching things with his bare hands: Freya's warrior sculpture, the cliff face he clambers down and the ice-cold face of Henry.

Finally, note that Simon had a career in insurance, another kind of protection. And in a sense, Bernard works in insurance as well — against a future he sees as inevitable.

Rabbits

'You will remember what happened to the rabbit,' says Bernard. If the accent hasn't given him away, this confirms that he's not a local. Rabbits, even simply mentioned in conversation, are considered bad luck on the Isle of Portland; in the heyday of stone quarrying there, workers often saw rabbits running from their warrens before a landslip, and considered them a bad omen. In *The Damned*, too, the rabbit is a kind of portent; its death mirrors that of two of the children.[22] If the bunker-world's reversals of logic recall, as I suggested, Lewis Carroll's topsy-turvy Wonderland, one can only guess at the fate that might have awaited the White Rabbit beneath Portland Bill.

Unicorns, replicants and mythical parents

The statue of the unicorn in the first sequence, as already mentioned, prefigures the radioactive children by evoking the idea of an impossible creature. Dig deeper into unicorn mythology, and one uncovers a few more resonances with the world of *The Damned*. It was a symbol of purity in the Middle Ages and its horn was believed to heal sickness and remove poison from drinking water — thus providing a cure for radiation sickness that occupies the same sphere of impossibility as the idea that Simon, Joan and King could contract it from the children in the first place. Incidentally, it was said that a unicorn could only be captured by a virgin; aptly enough, King, who Joan believes has never had sex, is the one lounging comfortably against it.

The presence of the unicorn also provides an irresistible opportunity to look at the influence of Losey's work on Ridley Scott. Because it doesn't stop at the unicorn/ *Blade Runner* connection: at least one writer, Vincent Joseph Noto, has traced a whole system of references to Losey in Scott's films. Discussing *The Damned*, Noto observes:

> The Replicants of *Blade Runner* obsess over their photographs. They seem to believe the photographs demonstrate that they are real humans by showing their early life, especially scenes of them with their parents. This motif is remarkably reminiscent of scenes depicting the pictures and photographs with which the radiation-immune children of *The Damned* have plastered the walls of their 'hideaway' cave. They too are obsessed with their parents and photographs or images which might depict their likeness. (2014)

In a further twist on the idea of confabulation and parenthood, a publicity photo taken on the set shows Shirley Anne Field posing with two of the children either side of her, and an open volume of the Encyclopaedia Britannica on her lap. All three are wreathed in smiles, looking for all the world like members of a nuclear family. It's as misleading an image as the publicity shots taken in the backstreets with the gang, but it wouldn't look out of place in the children's hideout, along with the other pictures of invented parents.

Names

Assigning a name is an act of authority and control; and in a film so concerned with authority and control, names and naming emerge as a recurring theme. This happens not just at the script level but in the surrounding discourse.

Simon's liberal-humanist exterior shows a crack or two when Joan, the morning after his mugging, points out that he doesn't even know her name. He replies: 'With a figure like that, you don't need a name.' Very noir, but out of place and jarringly crass (and reminiscent both of Losey's dismissive attitude towards Shirley Ann Field as a starlet forced on him by Hammer and Columbia, and of the character of Joan as strangely mutable and unfixed). A moment or two later, Simon casts her as Lady Godiva, and she retorts by naming him Peeping Tom. Enter King (self-christened, we have to assume), who starts calling him Simple Simon. Later, they meet a whole bunkerful of children named after English monarchs (the shooting script, in its rundown of their attributes, appoints Victoria 'leader of the group'), perhaps indicating Bernard's intention that they will emerge post-holocaust to rule the ruins. In a line cut from the finished film, one of the boys resets the whole naming process by suggesting that Simon and Joan are Adam and Eve; and if you know your Old Testament, you may recall that it was Adam who supposedly named all living creatures.

Losey's own name became a subject of contention in the wake of his troubles with McCarthyism; for the credits of his first few British films, he was unable to use his own name. His production designer on *The Damned* and frequent close collaborator, Richard MacDonald, had to work uncredited for years because he didn't have the right union membership. Think, also, of Losey's determination to call his film *The Brink*, and its eventual market-driven title of *The Damned* — to be changed again to *These Are The Damned* for the US release. For a director so vocal about his battles to maintain control over his work, and so preoccupied with power and its misuse, the idea of names and naming had a symbolic and political as well as a personal significance.

Helicopters

'On the very day that [he] died the place suddenly swarmed with helicopters,' says a colleague of the doomed journalist-hero Jonny Parks in Lawrence's *The Children of Light* (1960: 189). Mechanical vultures, indeed.

Sixties cinema swarmed with helicopters. Agile, sleekly modern and, in its ability to hover in one position, quite menacing, the helicopter could represent the emerging surveillance state, as in *The Damned*, or it could be employed as a playful signifier of post-war newness, as in the iconic opening sequence of *La Dolce Vita* (1960) or the singing-chopper-pilot premise of the Elvis Presley vehicle *Paradise, Hawaiian Style* (1966). Edith De Rham suggests that *The Damned* marks '...the first time anyone

Figure 13: King flees Bernard's bird

featured a helicopter as a "character" in a film' (1991: 122); whether or not this is true (and I can't think of an earlier example), one of the two Westland Whirlwind helicopters used for the production — G-ANFH, known as 'Sir Ector' — worked up a small filmography, appearing next in *A Hard Day's Night* (1964) and the Dean Martin vehicle *Murderer's Row* (1966). It's now gently disintegrating in a corner of the Helicopter Museum in Weston-super-Mare. Freya's revenge, perhaps, as its scarred form rots by the sea, not entirely unlike a Frink sculpture.[23]

Footnotes

22. In 2005, it was reported that Aardman Animations, out of respect for this belief, had produced special local promotional posters for *Wallace and Gromit and the Curse of the Were-Rabbit* (2005) that omitted the offending word and said instead 'Something bunny is going on'. See the BBC online news story (http://news.bbc.co.uk/1/hi/england/dorset/4318710.stm, accessed 1-5-2017).
23. A web search unexpectedly turned up the information in this paragraph; see www.hmfriends.org.uk/brisganfhbig.htm (Accessed 1-5-2017)

Filmography and Bibliography

Filmography

The following is a list of pertinent films cited throughout the text.

1930s

Pete Roleum and His Cousins (Joseph Losey, 1939)

Things to Come (William Cameron Menzies, 1936)

1940s

Boy with Green Hair, The (Joseph Losey, 1948)

Child Went Forth, A (Joseph Losey, 1941)

Diary for Timothy, A (Humphrey Jennings, 1945)

Fallen Idol, The (Carol Reed, 1948)

Gun in His Hand, A (Joseph Losey, 1945)

Hue and Cry (Charles Crichton, 1947)

Rocking Horse Winner, The (Anthony Pelissier, 1949)

Third Man, The (Carol Reed, 1949)

Words for Battle (Humphrey Jennings, 1941)

Youth Gets a Break (Joseph Losey, 1941)

1950s

Abominable Snowman, The (Val Guest, 1957)

Bad Seed, The (Mervyn LeRoy, 1956)

Big Night, The (Joseph Losey, 1951)

Blind Date (Joseph Losey, 1959)

Curse of Frankenstein, The (Terence Fisher, 1957)

Dracula (Terence Fisher, 1958)

Four-Sided Triangle (Terence Fisher, 1953)

Gamma People, The (John Gilling, 1956)

Glass Cage, The (Montgomery Tully, 1955)

Gypsy and the Gentleman, The (Joseph Losey, 1958)

Imbarco a mezzanotte (*Stranger on the Prowl*) (Joseph Losey, 1951)

Intimate Stranger, The (Joseph Losey, 1956)

Kiss Me Deadly (Robert Aldrich, 1955)

Lawless, The (Joseph Losey, 1950)

M (Joseph Losey, 1951)

On the Beach (Stanley Kramer, 1959)

Prowler, The (Joseph Losey, 1951)

Quatermass Xperiment, The (Val Guest, 1955)

Quatermass 2 (Val Guest, 1957)

Seven Days to Noon (John & Roy Boulting, 1950)

Seventh Seal, The (Ingmar Bergman, 1957)

Sleeping Tiger, The (Joseph Losey, 1954)

Spaceways (Terence Fisher, 1953)

Time Without Pity (Joseph Losey, 1957)

X: the Unknown (Leslie Norman, 1955)

1960s

Accident (Joseph Losey, 1967)

Beat Girl (Edmond T Gréville, 1960)

Bed Sitting Room, The (Richard Lester, 1969)

Boom! (Joseph Losey, 1968)

Children of the Damned (Anton M Leader, 1964)

Criminal, The (Joseph Losey, 1960)

Curse of the Werewolf, The (Terence Fisher, 1961)

Damned, The (Joseph Losey, 1963)

Day the Earth Caught Fire, The (Val Guest, 1961)

Dr Strangelove: Or, How I Learned to Stop Worrying and Love the Bomb (Stanley Kubrick, 1964)

Entertainer, The (Tony Richardson, 1960)

Eva (Joseph Losey, 1962)

Innocents, The (Jack Clayton, 1961)

King & Country (Joseph Losey, 1964)

Leather Boys (Sidney J Furie, 1964)

Maniac (Michael Carreras, 1963)

Modesty Blaise (Joseph Losey, 1966)

Moon Zero Two (Roy Ward Baker, 1969)

Nanny, The (Seth Holt, 1965)

Paranoiac (Freddie Francis, 1963)

Quatermass and the Pit (Roy Ward Baker, 1967)

Secret Ceremony (Joseph Losey, 1968)

Servant, The (Joseph Losey, 1963)

System, The (Michael Winner, 1964)

Village of the Damned (Wolf Rilla, 1960)

1970s

Clockwork Orange, A (Stanley Kubrick, 1971)

Figures in a Landscape (Joseph Losey, 1970)

Go-Between, The (Joseph Losey, 1971)

Romantic Englishwoman, The (Joseph Losey, 1975)

1980s

Blade Runner (Ridley Scott, 1982)

Bibliography

Brosnan, John (1978): *Future Tense: The Cinema of Science Fiction*. London: St Martin's Press.

Burstow, Robert (2014): 'Geometries of Hope and Fear: The Iconography of Atomic Science and Nuclear Anxiety in the Modern Sculpture of World War and Cold War Britain', in Jolivette, Catherine (ed.), *British Art in the Nuclear Age*. London: Ashgate.

Callahan, Dan (2003): *Joseph Losey*. Senses of Cinema (sensesofcinema.com). Accessed 29/09/2016.

Caute, David (1994): *Joseph Losey: A Revenge on Life*. London: Faber & Faber.

Ciment, Michel (ed.) (1985): *Conversations with Losey*. London: Methuen & Co Ltd.

Cohen, Stanley (2002): *Folk Devils and Moral Panics*, Third Edition. London: Routledge.

Conolly, Jez (2008): *Beached Margin: The role and representations of the seaside resort in British films*. Bristol: Jez Conolly.

De Rham, Edith (1991): *Joseph Losey*. London: Andre Deutsch Ltd.

Durgnat, Raymond (1970): *A Mirror for England*. London: Faber & Faber Ltd.

Elliott, Paul (2014): *Studying the British Crime Film*. Leighton Buzzard: Auteur Publishing.

Felleman, Susan (2014): *Real Objects in Unreal Situations: Modern Art in Fiction Films*. Chicago: University of Chicago Press.

Field, Shirley Anne (1991): *A Time for Love*. London: Bantam Press.

French, Philip (1963): 'Age of Violence', in *The Observer*, 19/05/1963: 27.

French, Philip (2013): 'Farewell, Philip French: the film critic's critic answers your questions', in *The Observer*, 25/08/2013. Accessed 07/08/2016.

Freud, Sigmund (1919/2003): 'The Uncanny', in *The Uncanny* (translated by David McLintock). London: Penguin Books.

Frink, Elisabeth (1985): 'In conversation with Sarah Kent', *ICA Talks*. Audio recording, 13 March 1985. British Library Sound Archive. Accessed 26 April 2017. http://sounds.bl.uk/Arts-literature-and-performance/ICA-talks/024M-C0095X0164XX-0100V0

Frink, Elisabeth (1992): 'Artists' Lives' interview with Sarah Kent, 28-29 December 1992. British Library transcript. Accessed 26 April 2017. http://sounds.bl.uk/related-content/TRANSCRIPTS/021T-C0466X0012XX-ZZZZA0.pdf

Gardiner, Stephen (1998): *Frink: The Official Biography of Elisabeth Frink*. London: Harper Collins.

Gardner, Colin (2004): *Joseph Losey*. Manchester: Manchester University Press.

Gaskin, Fiona (2014): 'The *Genius Loci* of Cold War Britain: The Metamorphic Landscapes of Graham Sutherland, Peter Lanyon and Alan Reynolds', in Jolivette, Catherine (ed.), *British Art in the Nuclear Age*. London: Ashgate.

Gow, Gordon (1971): 'Weapons: Joseph Losey in an interview with Gordon Gow' in *Films and Filming* Vol 18 no 1.

Harper, Sue and Porter, Vincent (2003): *British Cinema of the 1950s: The Decline of Deference*. Oxford: Oxford University Press.

Hearn, Marcus and Barnes, Alan (2007): *The Hammer Story: The Authorised History of Hammer Films*. London: Titan Books.

Hearn, Marcus (2010): *The Damned* (viewing notes for DVD reissue). London: Sony Pictures Home Entertainment.

Hogg, Jonathan (2016): *British Nuclear Culture*. London: Bloomsbury.

Holmes, Dennis: 'Strike robot is made in Germany', *Daily Mail* (London), 2 May 1956.

Houston, Penelope (1961): 'Conversations with Nicholas Ray and Joseph Losey', *Sight and Sound* vol 30, no 4.

Huckvale, David (2006): *James Bernard, Composer to Count Dracula: A Critical Biography*. Jefferson, NC: McFarland.

Hunter, IQ (ed.) (1999): *British Science Fiction Cinema*. London: Routledge.

Jacob, Gilles (1966): 'Joseph Losey, or The Camera Calls' in *Sight and Sound* vol 35, no 2.

Jacobi, Carol (2014): '"A Kind of Cold War Feeling" in British Art, 1945-1952', in Jolivette, Catherine (ed.), *British Art in the Nuclear Age*. London: Ashgate.

Kinsey, Wayne (2002): *Hammer Films: The Bray Studios Years*. London: Reynolds & Hearn Ltd.

Laucht, Christoph (2014): 'An Imagined Cataclysm Becomes Fact: British Photojournalism in Real and Imagined Nuclear War in Picture Post', in Jolivette, Catherine (ed.), *British Art in the Nuclear Age*. London: Ashgate.

Laurence, William L (1945): 'Eyewitness Account of Atomic Bomb Over Nagasaki', US War Department Press Release 9-9-1945. Online at the Atomic Archive. Accessed 30/4/17. www.atomicarchive.com/Docs/Hiroshima/Nagasaki.shtml

Lawrence, Herbert Lionel (1960): *The Children of Light*. London: Macdonald.

Mawston, Mark (2010): 'Field of dreams' (interview with Shirley Anne Field), in *Cinema Retro* vol 6: Issue 16.

Mayersberg, Paul (1963): 'Contamination', in *Movie* issue 9, May 1963.

McCamley, Nick (2007): *Cold War Secret Nuclear Bunkers: The Passive Defence of the Western World During the Cold War*. Barnsley: Pen & Sword Books Ltd.

Masco, Joseph (2006): *The Nuclear Borderlands: The Manhattan Project in Post-Cold War New Mexico*. Princeton: Princeton University Press.

Meikle, Denis (1996): *A History of Horrors: The Rise and Fall of the House of Hammer*. Lanham: Scarecrow Press.

Milne, Tom (ed.) (1968): *Losey on Losey*. London: Secker & Warburg.

Muller, Robert: 'Quatermass Speaking!', *Daily Mail* (London), 2 January 1959.

Murphy, Robert (1992): *Sixties British Cinema*. London: British Film Institute.

Newman, Kim (1999): *Millennium Movies: End of the World Cinema*. London: Titan Books Ltd.

Noto, Vincent Joseph (2014): 'Ridley's Key: The Forgotten Influence of Joseph Losey in *Blade Runner*'. *The Luminary* (lancaster.ac.uk/luminary/), issue 4. Accessed 09/04/2016.

Nuttall, Jeff (1968): *Bomb Culture*. London: MacGibbon & Kee Ltd.

Orwell, George (1945): 'You and the Atom Bomb', in Orwell, Sonia and Angus, Ian (eds) (1968), *The Collected Essays, Journalism and Letters of George Orwell, Volume IV: In Front of Your Nose*. London: Secker & Warburg Ltd.

Petley, Julian (1999): 'The Monstrous Child', in *The Body's Perilous Pleasures: Dangerous Desires and Contemporary Culture*, Michele Aaron (ed.), Edinburgh: Edinburgh University Press,

Pirie, David (2008): *A New Heritage of Horror*. London: IB Tauris & Co Ltd.

Porter, Vincent (1983): 'The Context of Creativity: Ealing Studios and Hammer Films', in James Curran and Vincent Porter (eds), *British Cinema History*. New Jersey: Barnes & Noble Books.

Powys, John Cowper (1934/1980): *Weymouth Sands*. London: Pan Books.

Rayner, Nicola (2008): 'Damning evidence of film-making process', *Dorset Echo*, 19 February. Accessed online 14 April 2017.

Salter, Gregory (2014): 'Cold War at Home: John Bratby, the Self and the Nuclear Threat', in Jolivette, Catherine (ed.), *British Art in the Nuclear Age*. London: Ashgate.

Shaw, Tony (2006): *British Cinema and the Cold War: The State, Propaganda and Consensus*. London: IB Tauris & Co Ltd.

Sandbrook, Dominic (2006): *Never Had It So Good: A History of Britain from Suez to the Beatles*. London: Abacus.

Sanjek, David (2002): *Cold, Cold Heart: Joseph Losey's The Damned and the Compensations of Genre*. Senses of Cinema (sensesofcinema.com). Accessed 08/04/2016.

Sarris, Andrew (1968): *The American Cinema: Directors and Directions 1929-1968*. New York: EP Dutton.

Sinyard, Neil (2003): 'Intimate Stranger: the early British films of Joseph Losey', in Ian MacKillop and Neil Sinyard (eds), *British Cinema of the 1950s: A Celebration*. Manchester: Manchester University Press.

Sontag, Susan (1965): 'The Imagination of Disaster', in *Commentary*, October 1965 pp42-48.

Winnicott, DW (1984): *Deprivation and Delinquency*. London: Tavistock Publications.